WISConsin
PORTRAITS

55 people who
made a difference

martin
hintz

TRAILS BOOKS
Black Earth, Wisconsin

Library of Congress Catalog Card Number: 00-100527
ISBN: 0-915024-80-2

Editor: Stan Stoga
Production and design: Impressions Book and Journal Services, Inc.
Cover design: Kate Orenberg

Printed in the United States of America.
06 05 04 03 02 01 00   6 5 4 3 2 1

Trails Books, a division of
Trails Media Group, Inc.
P.O. Box 317
Black Earth, WI 53515

(800) 236-8088   e-mail: info@wistrails.com
www.trailsbooks.com

Contents

INTRODUCTION 1

Jean Nicolet (1598–1642) explorer 2

Father Jacques Marquette (1637–1675) explorer.......................4

Charles de Langlade (1729–1801) soldier 6

Black Hawk (1767–1838) Native American leader 8

Marie Chevalier (1793?–1865) businesswoman 10

Stephen Bonga (1799?–1884) businessman and

    political leader 12

Increase Lapham (1811–1875) naturalist and historian............14

Nelson Dewey (1813–1889) politician 16

Alexander Mitchell (1817–1887) business leader and

    politician 18

Christopher Latham Sholes (1819–1890) inventor 20

William Dempster Hoard (1836–1918) dairyman 22

John Muir (1838–1914) environmentalist 24

H. H. Bennett (1843–1908) photographer 26

King Gillette (1855–1932) inventor and businessman.............28

Robert M. La Follette (1855–1925) politician.............30

Carrie Chapman Catt (1859–1947) suffrage leader.................32

Hamlin Garland (1860–1940) author......................................34

Theodora Winton Youmans (1863–1932) suffrage leader..........36

John R. Ringling (1866–1936) circus owner and businessman....38

Laura Ingalls Wilder (1867–1957) author...............................40

Frank Lloyd Wright (1867–1959) architect 42

Harry Houdini (1874–1926) magician 44

Zona Gale (1874–1938) author 46

William "Billy" Mitchell (1879–1936) aviator 48

Douglas MacArthur (1880–1964) soldier 50

William Harley (1880–1943) and Arthur Davidson (1881–1950)

    businessmen 52

Edna Ferber (1885–1968) journalist and author 54

Georgia O'Keefe (1887–1986) artist 56

Aldo Leopold (1887–1948) environmentalist 58

Alfred Lunt (1892–1977) and Lynn Fontanne (1887–1983)

    actors 60

Thornton Wilder (1897–1975) author....................................62

Golda Meir (1898–1978) world leader 64

Spencer Tracy (1900–1967) actor 66

Joseph McCarthy (1908–1957) politician 68

John Bardeen (1908–1991) scientist......................................70

Vince Lombardi (1913–1970) football coach...........................72

Woody Herman (1913–1987) musician 74

Orson Wells (1915–1985) actor and director 76

Gaylord Nelson (b. 1916) politican and environmentalist 78

Les Paul (b. 1916) musician..80

Liberace (1919–1987) entertainer 82

Vel Phillips (b. 1924) social activist......................................84

William Rehnquist (b. 1924) Supreme Court justice 86

John Colt (1925–1999) artist...88

James Lovell (b. 1928) astronaut 90

Father James Groppi (1930–1985) social activist 92

Alan Ameche (1933–1988) football player 94

Henry Aaron (b. 1934) baseball player 96

Ada Deer (b. 1935) political activist......................................98

Al Jarreau (b. 1940) jazz singer 100

Eric Heiden (b. 1958) and Beth Heiden (b. 1959)

    speed skaters 102

Brett Favre (b. 1969) football player....................................104

INDEX..106

PHOTO CREDITS 113

TIMELINE 114

Introduction

In this book, you will read about 55 special people who have some link to Wisconsin. Many were born in the state. Others moved here from elsewhere. They come in all ages, shapes, sizes, and colors. Some lived a long time ago and others are still alive today. Some you will recognize and others will be less familiar. Nearly all of them achieved goals that made the state, the country, or the world a better place. A few others are known for deeds that were not as noble.

These famous people include athletes, soldiers, entertainers, politicians, business leaders, reformers, and dreamers. They wrote books, composed music, broke athletic records, invented machines, helped others, or established successful businesses. They worked hard. They took advantage of all the opportunities they were offered. They were not quitters, even when the going was tough or when they were frightened and tired.

The personalities in this book are only a few of the hundreds of well-known people who have had some link to Wisconsin. And they do not include many others who may not have been famous but who achieved great things in their lifetime.

The people you will read about also reflect the history of Wisconsin. They show how the state has moved from a rugged wilderness to a thriving community made up of many different people. From the early explorers, to inventors and politicians, to today's athletes and social activists, its citizens have made a difference. They have changed and have been changed by the world around them.

Look around. Maybe the person sitting next to you will be famous some day . . . and so might you!

Jean Nicolet (1598–1642)

explorer

Jean Nicolet was a French explorer of North America's upper Midwest. Sometime in 1598, he was born in Cherbourg, France. As an eager young adventurer, he sailed to Canada with Samuel de Champlain in 1618. Nicolet then spent several years traveling through the wilderness. He learned the ways of the forest from the Native Americans who lived along the Ottawa River in what is now eastern Canada. He understood several languages and became an interpreter for French traders.

Nicolet was such a good friend of the Nipissing that they made him a member of their tribe, allowing him to sit in on their councils. His advice about how to deal with the Europeans made him a highly respected visitor. Always proud of his French heritage, Nicolet lived with the Nipissing while British troops occupied Quebec from 1629 to 1632. Since the city was one of Canada's major trade hubs, Nicolet then took a job there as a clerk for a fur company.

Because he knew the ways of the Native Americans so well, Nicolet often went with expeditions deep into the North American wilderness. In 1634, he traveled down Lake Michigan as far south as Green Bay. When Nicolet stepped ashore from his canoe, he wore a red silk robe and fired off two pistols to impress the Ho-Chunk people. At first some of the locals were scared, thinking Nicolet carried thunder in his hands. Shortly afterwards, however, more than 5,000 warriors attended a huge feast in his honor. He then explored the Fox River, canoeing as far south as Lake Winnebago, where he worked out a peace treaty with the Ho-Chunk who lived in the region.

The brave Nicolet spent a winter with the Ho-Chunk and learned the ways of other Native American nations who came through the area. Among them were the Sioux, Assiniboine, Illinois, and Potawatomi.

Wisconsin's total area covers 56,153 square miles. The longest north-south distance is 314 miles and the widest east-west distance is 293 miles.

When spring finally came in 1635, Nicolet went back to Quebec. He was full of stories about the rich opportunities for fur-trapping and trading in the territory he had visited. His careful accounts helped later explorers plan their journeys. And, because he worked for peaceful relations with all Native American tribes, they considered him a great friend.

Unfortunately, Nicolet drowned on November 1, 1642, while trying to rescue an Iroquois ally who had been captured by the Algonquins. ♦

Jean Nicolet's landing at Green Bay in 1634, shown in this 1904 oil painting by Edwin Deming

Father Jacques Marquette (1637–1675)

explorer

Father Jacques Marquette was a Jesuit priest who was always ready for an adventure. He is best known for helping French-Canadian explorer Louis Jolliet find the Mississippi River.

Long before that exciting trip, Marquette had learned a lot about the New World. He was born on June 1, 1637, in Lacn, France. After he came to North America as a missionary, he established several frontier churches. One of them was St. Ignace, north of the Straits of Mackinac in what is now Michigan. With his knowledge of Native Americans and their languages, Marquette was an excellent choice to join Jolliet.

The men spent the winter of 1672–73 at St. Ignace planning their expedition. In mid-May, the ice broke up on the rivers flowing south, allowing them to depart. They and five companions traveled simply, carrying only some corn and smoked meat to eat. It "was a glorious undertaking," Marquette wrote in his journal.

Father Marquette, with Louis Jolliet, pictured here in an oil painting by Robert Thom

Saint Joan of Arc, who lived in France in the fifteenth century, is thought to have prayed in a chapel brought to the campus of Marquette University in Milwaukee and rebuilt.

The men traveled along the north shore of Lake Michigan, through Green Bay and down the Fox River to the Wisconsin River, into "strange lands," said the fearless priest. It took another 100 miles of paddling before they reached the rolling, muddy waters of the Mississippi River on June 17.

The party traveled on for another month, exploring the great river as far south as the mouth of the Arkansas River. Worried about unfriendly Native Americans and the possibility that the Spanish were nearby, they decided to turn back. After a great deal of struggle, they made it to the St. Francis Xavier mission at De Pere, now a suburb of Green Bay.

Marquette stayed at the mission for a year to rest and write his journal about the trip. The book was published in 1681. Once that task was completed, he set out on more missionary work among the Illinois people. But Marquette never fully recovered from the hardships of his long trip to the Mississippi. He became ill and died in 1675. His body was carried back to his beloved St. Ignace for burial.

Years later, several of his bone fragments were given to Marquette University, a college in Milwaukee named in his honor. Several cities, counties, rivers, and a railroad are also named after him. Statues of the explorer-priest stand in the Capitol in Washington, D.C. Another is outside the Wisconsin Division of Tourism information center at Prairie du Chien.

The Marquette-Jolliet expedition was important because it helped open the way for other explorers to find their way into the heart of North America. ♦

Charles de Langlade (1729–1801)

soldier

Charles Michel de Langlade is often called the "Father of Wisconsin" because he was one of the first permanent white residents in the area. He was born in Mackinac, Michigan, sometime in May 1729. His mother was the daughter of an Ottawa tribal leader. His father was a French trader. Langlade therefore had the best of two worlds. He knew the ways of the Native Americans, as well as those of the Europeans.

When he was only 10 years old, Langlade traveled down the Mississippi River in a trading party made up of his Ottawa relatives. On the way, they met some French soldiers canoeing upriver from their base in New Orleans. From then on, Langlade was certain he wanted to be a soldier. In 1745 he arrived in Green Bay with his father to help set up and run a trading post. But Langlade was not content being a shopkeeper.

When he was old enough, he joined the French colonial army. In the middle of the 1700s, the frontier was exciting and dangerous. One of the reasons was that both the British and French wanted control of the fur trade. There were also disputes over the boundaries of their colonies.

The British moved into Ohio and built a fort in an area that the French considered their territory. Langlade was sent to get rid of the intruders in 1752. He captured the fort in a bloody battle that was one of the first steps toward the French and Indian War of 1754.

With his knowledge of both French and Native American ways, Langlade rallied Wisconsin's Native Americans toward the French cause. He went to Pennsylvania with the French army and defeated the British in several battles. However, the British finally won the war. They took Canada and all the French lands east of the Mississippi River, an area that included the Wisconsin territory.

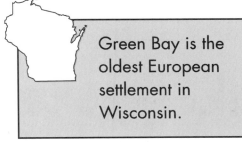

Green Bay is the oldest European settlement in Wisconsin.

After the war, the British were suspicious of Langlade. They ignored his warnings of possible attack by the Native American. This careless view resulted in the deaths of many British soldiers and settlers. So Langlade returned to Green Bay, where he hoped to retire quietly. The American Revolution, however, changed his plans. He again offered to serve with the British, who finally realized that a man with his military and frontier experience would be valuable. He was accepted into the British army and fought many battles against the rebellious Americans.

With the victory of the American colonists, he returned again to Green Bay, where he finally got his wish to live quietly on his homestead. He died around July 26, 1801, although the records are not specific.

Langlade County in northeastern Wisconsin is named after this brave soldier who fought for two different countries and helped settle a third one. ◆

Charles de Langlade, shown here about 1735 at his trading post at Green Bay

Black Hawk (1767–1838)
Native American leader

Black Hawk was a subchief of the Sac (sometimes spelled as Sauk) nation. He was born in 1767 and grew up in Saukenuk, a village in central Illinois.

Black Hawk fondly remembered his years there as a youngster fishing, hunting, and learning the ways of his people. The young man also learned the art of war by raiding the Osage, Sioux, and Cherokees. These people were the traditional enemies of the Sac.

After the American Revolution, Yankee settlers poured into the heartland of the newly established United States. The arrivals wanted all the Native Americans to be pushed west of the Mississippi. Hoping for peace, the Sac chiefs signed a treaty. However, they did not understand the white man's concept of land ownership. The chiefs thought that the treaty only meant that they were not to wage war with the whites. But under the agreement, the Sac actually gave their lands east of the Mississippi to the United States.

Black Hawk always thought that his people were not treated fairly by the American government. But after being a war chief for so long, he wanted to retire peacefully on the land that he loved. He decided to move into Iowa, where he felt safe.

In 1832, he and his followers fled through Wisconsin, hoping to cross the Mississippi River into Iowa near Prairie du Chien. But they suffered

Black Hawk, pictured in an oil painting done by Charles Bird King around 1837

Corporal Mitchell Red Cloud, of Hatfield, Wisconsin, was the nation's first Native American to receive the Medal of Honor, the country's highest award for bravery. During the Korean War in 1950, he courageously fought off a large enemy attack to give his fellow troops time to regroup. He died during the action.

from a lack of food and shelter. Many old people, children, and the sick and wounded died along the way. There was no chance to rest because they were being chased by the army. History books call this the Black Hawk War.

The soldiers caught up with them on July 21, and a battle was fought on Wisconsin Heights. This area is west of the current city of Madison. The battlefield is now called the Black Hawk Unit of the Lower Wisconsin Riverway. A pleasant park there has a trail tracing the fighting that occurred so many years ago.

Some of the Sac managed to make it to the nearby Mississippi River. The few who got across were murdered by Sioux hiding on the opposite bank. A plaque noting this tragedy was erected on the Wisconsin side of the river in 1990. Wisconsin Governor Tommy Thompson made a formal apology to the modern-day Sac people for what was done to their ancestors.

Black Hawk was captured and sent to prison in Fort Monroe, Virginia. While in jail, he told his story to a government official. The book that was a result is considered an American classic. It tells of life on the frontier from the Native American point of view. At the conclusion of his story, Black Hawk urged peace and friendship between the white man and the Sac nation.

After his release, Black Hawk returned to the Midwest and lived on a reservation near the Des Moines River in Iowa. He died on October 3, 1838. ◆

Marie Chevalier (1793?–1865)

businesswoman

Marie Chevalier could not read or write but she knew how to manage a store. For many years, she operated a trading post at the mouth of the Menominee River in northeastern Wisconsin. When she was a child, Marie was nicknamed Marie Antoinette after her grandmother. And her grandmother was named after the queen of France who held power just before the French Revolution. Soon young Marie's nickname evolved, or changed, into Queen Marinette.

It is believed that Marie Chevalier was born around 1793 at Post Lake, deep in the woods of northern Wisconsin. She was the granddaughter of Great Marten, a local Native American leader, and the daughter of a French-Canadian fur trader named Bartelemi Chevalier. Her family moved to Green Bay when her father opened a trading post there.

Soon after, in 1800, John Jacobs became a partner with the elder Chevalier. The girl fell in love with Jacobs, and they were married when she was 14. The couple had three children. When Jacobs opened another

The American Fur Company trading post at Fond du Lac, similar to the one operated by Marie Chevalier

trading post, Queen Marinette agreed to take care of business while he was on fur-buying trips. That was how she began to run the trading post.

On one trip deep into Canada, Jacobs disappeared. He may have been killed or died of an illness. No one knew for sure. So Queen Marinette had to keep working at the trading post to support her family. After a few years, William Farnsworth, another fur trader, came into her life. He was a dashing, handsome fellow, and the two were married. They also had three children.

Farnsworth worked for the American Fur Company, so he was also away from home a great deal. Queen Marinette did not seem to mind, and she continued to operate her store. Being very fair and honest, she was widely respected throughout the area. She was unlike some other traders, who often stole from natives and settlers alike. With her Native American heritage, she encouraged everyone to get along with each other, no matter what their skin color or family background.

When he finally settled down after years of traveling, Farnsworth built a sawmill. Using fresh boards from the mill, he built Queen Marinette the first frame house in northeast Wisconsin. Since the mill was a success, Farnsworth built a second one in Sheboygan. He was again gone for long periods of time.

In his absence, Queen Marinette ran her store with the help of her children. She finally retired and turned the business over to a son. But Queen Marinette stayed active, supplying fruit and vegetables for the post. Over the years, it became known as Marinette's. Today, it is the site of Marinette, Wisconsin. Marinette County is also named after this remarkable frontier woman.

Marie Chevalier, Queen Marinette, died on June 3, 1865, and is buried in Green Bay. ◆

Stephen Bonga (1799?–1884)
businessman and political leader

Stephen Bonga, one of the first known blacks in Wisconsin, was the grandson of slaves. From their humble beginning, the Bongas (who are also known as the Bungos) became one of the most noted pioneer families in the upper Midwest. Highly respected merchants and community leaders, they were also very active in politics.

Stephen's grandfather and grandmother, Jean and Marie Jeanne Bonga, were owned by the British commander of Fort Mackinac, Michigan. In the 1700s, the fort was the Midwest's key military outpost. It was located on Mackinac Island, which lies in the Straits of Mackinac. This is a body of water that links Lakes Huron and Michigan.

When their owner, Captain Daniel Robertson, died in 1787, the Bongas were freed. They then ran the first private inn on Mackinac Island. The island, with its hotels and fort, is now popular with tourists.

Stephen's father, Pierre, was born around 1760. Pierre Bonga worked for the Northwest Fur Company, hauling furs from trading posts to markets in Canada. He became a trader himself at Fort St. Lewis, now Superior, Wisconsin. Pierre married an Ojibwa woman, and the couple had several children, one of whom was Stephen.

Because early records were not complete, it is not certain whether Bonga was born in 1799 or 1800. His father wanted him to receive a good education. So young Bonga was sent to Albany, New York, to study for the Presbyterian ministry. When he returned to Superior, Bonga did not want to be a preacher. So he opened his own trading post. It quickly became one of the largest in the region.

Bonga did not always stay behind the counter of his store. He was also a frontier guide and an Army interpreter, working with various native tribes. He was also a peacemaker. Upon learning that the Sioux

The city of Superior's maritime museum is actually a ship, a whaleback freighter named the SS *Meteor*. The ship, which once carried cargo across the Great Lakes, is moored in the harbor on Barker's Island.

were going to attack the Ojibwa, he traveled for four days by canoe up the St. Croix and Snake Rivers to warn missions and settlements of the danger. As a result, many lives were saved. During the 1863 Sioux uprising in Minnesota, Bonga joined the Wisconsin militia. He was more than 60 years old at the time!

Bonga was always involved in some project to improve the town of Superior. In 1881, his training as a minister paid off when he organized the Methodist Episcopal Church there. Years before, he had been one of the original signers of a petition asking for a new territorial government west of Lake Michigan. At the time, Wisconsin was part of Michigan. Through the efforts of Bonga and the others who presented the document to the authorities, Wisconsin became a separate territory in 1836.

Stephen Bonga

He died in 1884. The Bonga family, including many of his descendants, continues to live in northern Wisconsin. And Stephen was not the only notable one in the family. His brother, George, moved to the Minnesota frontier as a young man and also became a well-known political figure. Bonga Township in Cass County, Minnesota, is named after the family. ♦

Increase Lapham (1811–1875)
naturalist and historian

When Increase Allen Lapham arrived here in 1836, Wisconsin was still a territory. By the time he died in 1857, he had directed the state's growth in many cultural and scientific arenas. He helped found the Milwaukee Public Library, the Wisconsin Academy of Sciences, Arts and Letters, the State Historical Society of Wisconsin, the National Weather Service, and several schools.

Lapham also wrote more than 75 books on history, geology, and botany. Known around the world for his detailed studies of plants and animals, he provided research that helped later scholars. Lapham was born on March 7, 1811, near Macedon, New York. He was named after his mother's father, Increase Allen. His father was a contractor, whose specialty was building canals. These were long channels of water on which large boats transported freight and passengers in the days before highways or railroads.

Lapham's family moved frequently to wherever his father found work. Because of these moves, Lapham received little formal schooling. He had to educate himself through reading. But by the time he was 13, he was already collecting and studying rocks as an amateur geologist. When

Increase Lapham

14

Glaciers dug out 7,000 lakes in Wisconsin during the Ice Age thousands of years ago. There are at least 15,000 named inland lakes in the state, as well as 2,400 streams and rivers. Lake Winnebago is the state's largest lake, covering 215 square miles. Green Lake is the deepest, at 237 feet.

he was 15, Lapham was writing long letters to the scientists of his era. He carefully described what he saw on his hiking trips into the hills and strolls along the riverbanks. Lapham's first article on geology was published when he was only 16.

With only $16 in his pocket, Lapham came to the Wisconsin Territory to take a job as a surveyor. This is a person who measures boundaries for plots of land. He became Milwaukee's first register of claims, recording who owned what land. Even with all his work, Lapham enjoyed traveling to see the natural wonders of the vast new territory.

He appreciated what he saw of the land, which had barely been touched by farmers' plows and loggers' saws. It still contained great stands of white pine forests and pure, clear lakes. After a while, Lapham became keenly interested in saving this natural beauty for future generations. Under his strong guidance, the Wisconsin legislature passed the state's first two environmental laws. The first, in 1868, protected trees. The second, in 1875, dealt with rules on raising fish.

This busy scientist was also fascinated by Native American cultures. So he studied ancient earthen mounds built by mysterious residents of Wisconsin hundreds and hundreds of years ago. In addition, his daily observations on the state's ever-changing weather helped predict rain, storms, and snow. Through his efforts, he became known as the father of the National Weather Service.

Lapham died of a stroke on September 14, 1875, while fishing on Oconomowoc Lake. His friends said it was a fitting way for him to die, doing what he loved in the wide outdoors. ◆

Nelson Dewey (1813–1889)

politician

Nelson Dewey was the first governor of the state of Wisconsin. However, he was not native to the Midwest. He was born in Lebanon, Connecticut, on December 19, 1813, and grew up in Butternuts, New York. After he attended an academy, a kind of private high school, in Hamilton, New York, he taught school for a year.

Seeking adventure and opportunity, he moved to the rugged territory of Wisconsin. Settling in Lancaster, Dewey decided to become a lawyer. He quickly became active in politics. Dewey was elected Grant County's first registrar of deeds, the person who recorded settlers' property lines.

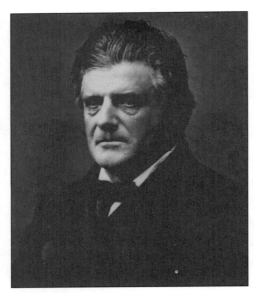

Nelson Dewey

He did such a good job as registrar and knew so many people that he was sent to the territorial legislative assembly in 1838. Dewey soon became the assembly's speaker. During its 1842–46 session, he was elected its president.

When Wisconsin became a state in 1848, Dewey was elected governor. He was reelected in 1850. He was also a good businessman, helping develop the lead-mining industry near his home along the Mississippi River. In addition, he operated a large successful farm. Many of the financial systems he put into place for Wisconsin during these early years are still in effect.

But running the state did not occupy all his time. Dewey still found plenty of time to court Kate Dunn, daughter of Charles Dunn, the territorial chief justice of Wisconsin. They were married during Dewey's first term in the governor's office. Their beautiful wedding was the talk of the state's social set for years.

Dewey took a break from politics between 1852 and 1854 but just could not stay away from the excitement. He became a state senator and was a commissioner for the state prison system from 1874 to 1881. Finally, after years of serving the state as a public official, Dewey retired to run his farm. However, he remained interested in helping the state grow. He was a delegate to the state conventions of the Democratic Party and a presidential elector in 1888.

Dewey was also active in many social causes and had a keen interest in history. He was elected president of the Wisconsin Historical Society in 1849. In 1853, it was chartered as the State Historical Society of Wisconsin.

He died in Cassville on July 21, 1889. His home there is now a popular state park. ◆

Alexander Mitchell (1817–1887)
business leader and politician

Alexander Mitchell always had big plans. He dreamed of big banks and big railroads. He was a businessman who took big chances to realize his big dreams. He was born on October 18, 1817, in Scotland. At age 22, he came to the United States to become secretary of the Wisconsin Marine & Fire Insurance Company. The business became a bank shortly after Mitchell began working there. He helped build Wisconsin Marine into a financial powerhouse in Wisconsin's early years. After a time, Mitchell bought out his partners and became president of the bank.

During the Civil War, some banks in the North had financial problems because they worked with banks in the South, which had broken away from the Union. But Mitchell was a shrewd businessman

Alexander Mitchell

who always seemed to be able to keep and make money. He was able to transfer millions of dollars worth of Wisconsin war bonds into the state's strongest banks. (A bond is a financial document issued by a government or business that pays interest, or extra money, to someone who buys it.) Mitchell's plan helped the banks stay open during the war. With such creative ideas like this, he later became the first president of the Wisconsin Banker's Association.

Wisconsin became the thirtieth state of the Union on May 29, 1848. It was the last state made from the territory east of the Mississippi River.

Mitchell is most famous for developing the railroad system in the state and the Midwest. In the 1850s, he was on the board of directors of the Milwaukee & St. Paul Railroad. When it was facing financial trouble, all its directors except Mitchell wanted to shut it down. He did not want to give up, saying that the railroad would remain a good business if it had better management. "Prove it," said the other directors.

So Mitchell did. When he became president of the Milwaukee & St. Paul in 1865, he had it making money within a year. When he took over, it operated only 270 miles of track. When he died on April 19, 1887, the line had more than 5,000 miles of track in Wisconsin, Illinois, Minnesota, Iowa, and South Dakota. The railroad was important in opening the upper Midwest to settlement.

Mitchell also loved politics. At first, he belonged to an early political party called the Whigs. He then joined the Republican Party. When President Abraham Lincoln was assassinated after the Civil War, Mitchell switched to the Democratic Party. He ran for the U.S. Congress in 1868 but was defeated. Successful on his second attempt in 1870, Mitchell was reelected in 1872.

Wisconsin Democrats wanted Mitchell to run for governor in 1877, but he wished to retire. So Mitchell thanked his supporters but refused to run. His son, John L. Mitchell, was a U.S. senator from Wisconsin from 1893 to 1899.

The ornate old Mitchell Building in Milwaukee, where the banker and railroad executive had his offices, remains one of the city's downtown landmarks. Mitchell, South Dakota, is also named after this hardworking businessman. ◆

Christopher Latham Sholes

(1819–1890)

inventor

Every time you use a computer keyboard, you can thank Christopher Latham Sholes. That's because, nearly 150 years ago, he helped develop the typewriter, which allowed people to create written messages more quickly and efficiently.

Sholes was born on February 14, 1819, the son of a cabinetmaker in Mooresburg, Pennsylvania. His mother died when he was only 7 years old. At age 14, Sholes left home to learn the printing trade. One of his first jobs was making type for the printing press. This work took a lot of time, and the boy began thinking of a better way to put words on paper.

In 1837, Sholes moved with his family to Green Bay because one of his brothers, a news-paperman, lived there. Already a master printer, Sholes got a job at the paper. He became an editor when he was 19. To bring in extra money, the paper printed important legal documents, including material for the Wisconsin Territorial Legislature. Young Sholes was in charge of making sure that it was all printed properly.

Christopher Latham Sholes

The first newspaper in Wisconsin was the *Green Bay Intelligencer*, founded by Albert G. Ellis in 1823.

With this experience, he moved to Kenosha and set up his own newspaper. There he became interested in politics. In 1845, Sholes was named the Kenosha postmaster. Elected a state senator from Kenosha County, he served in the Wisconsin Legislature from 1852 to 1853 and from 1856 to 1857. Sholes was an active reform candidate. That meant he supported causes ranging from women's rights to banning the drinking of alcohol. Sholes also hated slavery and introduced a law in the legislature protecting runaway slaves.

In 1860, Sholes moved to Milwaukee and got back into the newspaper business. He was an editor at the *Milwaukee News* and the *Milwaukee Daily-Sentinel*. But he could not stay away from politics. President Abraham Lincoln made him a customs officer in the Port of Milwaukee and he was appointed to Milwaukee's Board of Public Works.

All this time, Sholes believed that people would appreciate a fast and effective way of writing messages. So he and some friends designed a typing machine in 1868. His partners soon lost interest in the project, so Sholes kept working alone. He developed more than 50 models of the machine over the next several years. In the early 1870s, he felt satisfied enough to sell his idea to the Remington Arms Company for $12,000.

Sholes kept making improvements to his machine. With his first devices, typists needed to look at the keys when they worked. But to help a blind Civil War veteran, Sholes came up with the touch system of typing used today. This made it easier for such individuals—and for everyone—to use the device.

The inventor died on February 17, 1890 and is buried in Milwaukee's Forest Home Cemetery. A marker telling of Sholes's typewriter invention is located across the street from the home of today's *Milwaukee Journal Sentinel* newspaper. ♦

William Dempster Hoard

(1836–1918)

dairyman and politician

Probably the one person most responsible for making Wisconsin into "America's Dairyland" is William Dempster Hoard. A farmer, preacher, newspaperman, state governor, and educator, he was tireless in his efforts to further the state's dairy industry.

Hoard was born in the community of Stockbridge, New York, on October 10, 1836. His grandfather, a long-time dairy farmer, taught him the best way to make cheese and butter. Seeking work, he came to Wisconsin in 1857. Hoard became a farmer and augmented his income by teaching music. He was also a traveling Methodist preacher serving many small churches.

When the Civil War broke out, Hoard joined the Union infantry. He was wounded in 1862 but reenlisted and finished as a private in an artillery company. After the war, Hoard returned to Wisconsin. He eagerly looked forward to the peace and quiet of the state's pastures and fields.

In 1870, he started publishing the *Jefferson County Union*, a weekly newspaper. In his columns, he encouraged farmers to raise dairy cattle. He knew that this was a profitable

William Dempster Hoard

Wisconsin produces more than two million pounds of cheese each year. This is about 30 percent of the country's total cheese production, ranking Wisconsin first in the United States. Wisconsin dairies developed colby and brick cheeses, among the most popular brands in the nation. Many Wisconsin natives of Italian descent helped the state become one of the largest producers of Italian-style cheese in the country.

venture. Always encouraging new farming methods and farming causes, he also formed several dairy associations. In 1885, he launched *Hoard's Dairyman*, an agricultural magazine that is still published today.

To assist Wisconsin farmers in getting their dairy goods to market, Hoard encouraged railroads to give better freight rates to the dairymen. He also encouraged the use of silos to store cattle feed. These tall, round structures are seen on most farms today. He also knew it was important to protect the soil, so he supported planting alfalfa in farm fields. This crop added nitrogen to the earth, making it more productive. Hoard also wanted farmers to regularly test cattle for their health.

Hoard, a Republican, was elected governor of Wisconsin 1888. During the campaign, he was known as the Jersey Cow Candidate because of his knowledge of cattle! While governor, he supported the formation of the Dairy and Food Commission, a state office that looked after the quality of Wisconsin's agricultural products.

However, Hoard lost his reelection bid because he favored a law that required children to attend school. This angered many businessmen, who wanted to use cheap child labor. He also wanted all courses taught in English. Since many people in Wisconsin spoke German and various Scandinavian languages, they also voted against him.

Yet Hoard remained active in public life as president of the University of Wisconsin Board of Regents. He died on November 22, 1918, in Fort Atkinson. The town is now home to the Hoard Historical Museum and Dairy Shrine. For all his work, Hoard is known as the Father of Modern Dairying. ◆

John Muir (1838–1914)

environmentalist

The rush of prairie wind, the scent of oak leaves, the fresh feel of a cool, deep trout stream . . . all these were special to John Muir. He was one of the country's first citizens to actively promote clean air, water, and land. Muir loved nature and wanted it protected. As a result of his research, writings, and enthusiastic speeches, the U.S. government created some of its first environmental policies.

It is a bit strange to note, however, that Muir was not a native of this country. He was born in Dunbar, Scotland, on April 21, 1838. When he was a youngster, his father brought him to Wisconsin. Along with his sister, Sarah, and brother, David, Muir helped plow and plant their first homestead near Portage. When he was older, he wrote about his adventures as a frontier farm boy in the book *The Story of My Boyhood and Youth*, published in 1913.

As a youngster, Muir hoed weeds, built fences, and milked cows. While he worked, he studied the birds, plants, and animals all around him. In the evening, he read every book he could find. This was hard because his father got him up early to work in the fields. Even without much of a formal education, Muir entered the

John Muir

The state's highest waterfall is the Black River's Big Manitou Falls in Pattison State Park. The waterfall, in northwestern Wisconsin, drops 165 feet.

University of Wisconsin. Yet he left school in 1863 because he wanted to select his own courses. He did not want to be told what classes to take.

He spent the next years of his life walking around Wisconsin and visiting other states in the Midwest. Muir went to Canada and journeyed down to the Gulf of Mexico. He kept a detailed journal of everything he saw along the way, from the color of flowers to the size of bugs. He left nothing out.

He then traveled to California, Utah, and Alaska. He explored Yosemite Valley and many other rugged places in the frontier West. On his journeys, he worried about what he saw happening to the environment. Too many sheep were destroying the pastures in the Far West. In the north, vast areas of woods were being cleared by loggers. Not even a twig was left standing after the lumberjacks were finished.

Through these observations, Muir helped many people learn about the country's outdoor wonders. In his writings, lectures, and appeals to Congress, he battled businesses that did not care about the land. He took President Theodore Roosevelt on a camping trip and showed him the challenges facing the country's environment. As a result, Roosevelt set aside thousands of acres of parkland to be protected for future generations.

Although he did not pursue honors, Muir received many awards for his hard work on behalf of conserving the environment. He died on December 24, 1914, in Los Angeles, California. ♦

H. H. Bennett (1843–1908)
photographer

Called the Father of Wisconsin Tourism, H. H. Bennett took black-and-white photographs in the mid and late 1800s that showed the beauty of the Wisconsin Dells. Bennett took pictures of the area long before it became a popular vacation spot, with water slides and wax museums. Bennett wanted to record the natural wonders of central Wisconsin and the lives of the people there. His magnificent photos attracted international attention for their creativity, focus, and precision.

Born on January 15, 1843, Bennett came to Wisconsin from Canada. He dreamed of being a carpenter. The Civil War broke out, however, so he joined the Union army. He was wounded in the right hand when his gun accidentally discharged.

H. H. Bennett

He did not let his war injury slow him down, even though he had only a thumb and one finger on his hand. Bennett took up photography and made his own cameras. They were heavy, clumsy devices that stood on tripods, or three legs, far more difficult to use than today's point-and-shoot cameras.

Bennett rode giant log rafts down the Wisconsin River to take photos of how timber was transported to the sawmills before railroads took over the

Miners in western Wisconsin burrowed into the sides of hills looking for lead in the 1840s. They also often lived in hollowed-out caves like badgers, earning Wisconsin its nickname as the Badger State.

job. He stood at the edge of cliffs to take pictures of rock formations. Bennett crawled deep into caves. He rowed a small boat on the fast-flowing Wisconsin. He took many other chances to capture the right images. Bennett also took photos of the local Winnebago people, now known as the Ho-Chunk. Their ancestors had lived in the Dells area for centuries. His photos show them as a proud, handsome people.

He sold hundreds of pictures, many of which were used in stereoscopes. These were small handheld devices that allowed people to view photos with a three-dimensional effect. Remember, this was long before television and movies! Everyone became excited about the Wisconsin Dells and many people wanted to visit there. So they came . . . by the hundreds, by the thousands, soon by the tens of thousands. His photos helped make the Dells the attraction it is today. He died on January 1, 1908.

Bennett's renovated studio in downtown Wisconsin Dells is now a museum, operated by the State Historical Society of Wisconsin. Dozens of his photos are exhibited there, still attracting attention, just as they had more than a century ago. His former home on Oak Street is now a bed and breakfast. ◆

King Gillette (1855–1932)
inventor and businessman

King Camp Gillette was really sharp. One of his inventions was a razor that used disposable blades.

Gillette was born on January 5, 1855, in Fond du Lac. He was the fifth of seven children born to George Wolcott Gillette and Fanny Lemira Camp. Although his family moved to Chicago when Gillette was a youngster, some of his distant relatives still live in the Fond du Lac area.

After graduating from school, he became a traveling salesman. But in between his road trips, Gillette loved to tinker and make things in his home workshop. Gillette became a well-known inventor, taking out several patents dealing with such devices taps, valves, and faucets. A patent is an official document giving a person sole permission to manufacture or sell a product.

King Gillette

In 1895, his employer suggested that he invent something that could be used and then thrown away. This practice would keep customers returning to buy additional products.

One morning, Gillette woke up and wandered into his bathroom to shave. But the razor's single edge was too dull to do a good shearing job on his chin whiskers. Rather than taking the razor to a barber to be sharpened, a practice

The many paper products made in Wisconsin include tissue paper, cardboard boxes, copier paper, and paper bags. Green Bay is nicknamed the Toilet Paper Capitol of the World. There are many paper mills in the Fox River Valley and along the Wisconsin River.

common back then, he came up with the idea of throwaway blades. He figured that they could be thrown away when they became dull. He thought of using a thin blade of steel that was sharpened on both edges. A handle would clamp them together and prevent the user from cutting his fingers. There it was! The Gillette razor was born. The year was 1895.

Engineers told Gillette, however, that it was impossible to develop such an item because no one could build a machine to produce large numbers of sharpened blades. But he found a craftsman who could do it. Gillette soon left his employer and became president of his own firm in 1901. His company was called the American Safety Razor Company.

A year later, the company was renamed the Gillette Safety Razor Co. The idea of disposable razors caught on when the government issued his razors to troops during World War I. The Fond du Lac native remained president of the company until 1931 and was a director until his death on July 9, 1932, in Los Angeles.

He was also a social reformer, believing that a worldwide corporation owned by ordinary people holding shares of stock in the company would help overcome poverty. He described his ideas in books such as *The Human Drift* (1894), *The Ballot Box* (1897), and *Gillette's Social Redemption* (1900).

Gillette razor blades are still very popular, used by nearly everyone who shaves. And his company, now called simply the Gillette Company, has grown into a huge corporation that makes and sells many other consumer products. ◆

Robert M. La Follette (1855–1925)

politician

Robert M. La Follette was proud to be born in a log cabin. From this humble beginning, he became one of Wisconsin's best-known and beloved government leaders. He was born on June 14, 1855, in Primrose, a village in central Wisconsin. His parents were farmers whose ancestors came from Europe around 1750. The older La Follettes lived in Kentucky and Indiana before coming to the Wisconsin frontier. In Kentucky, they lived near Abraham Lincoln's family.

Young La Follette was used to working hard. He chopped wood, planted crops, and looked after the farm livestock, but he did not want to be a farmer. He earned enough money to attend the University of

Robert M. La Follette

Wisconsin and became a lawyer. He quickly earned a reputation as a debater and a great speaker. While in school, La Follette met his future wife, Belle Case, who was to become a great influence on him throughout his political career.

La Follette, a Republican, was elected Dane County district attorney in 1880. He was elected to the U.S. Congress in 1884, serving until 1891. After he was defeated, La Follette returned to Madison to practice law. But he was determined to

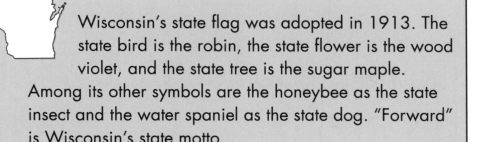

Wisconsin's state flag was adopted in 1913. The state bird is the robin, the state flower is the wood violet, and the state tree is the sugar maple. Among its other symbols are the honeybee as the state insect and the water spaniel as the state dog. "Forward" is Wisconsin's state motto.

reform govern-ment, especially to free state politics from the control of corrupt party bosses. Of course, this got him into trouble with the head of the Republican Party. Although he hoped to be the party's candidate for governor, La Follette was not nominated. He was too outspoken. In fact, he was so fiery that he became known as "Fighting Bob."

However, he could not keep away from the political scene. He decided to run again for governor in 1900. This time he was successful, becoming the first Wisconsin governor to have been born in the state. His ideas for improving state government were called the Wisconsin Idea. They included tax and election reforms and state control of the railroads. Many other states liked what they saw in Wisconsin and used his ideas for their own reforms.

La Follette carried his courage and high ideals with him to Washington when he was elected to the U.S. Senate in 1906. He served until 1925, becoming a powerful Senate leader during his several terms in office. A group of political activists, the Progressives, encouraged La Follette to run for president in 1924. He accepted their nomination and actually received five million votes in that year's election. But it was not quite enough to win the presidency, so he returned to the Senate.

Tired and ill after his presidential race, La Follette died on June 18, 1925, in Washington, D.C. He was followed in the Senate by his oldest son, Robert M. La Follette Jr. ♦

Carrie Chapman Catt

(1859–1947)

suffrage leader

Women in this country have been allowed to vote only since August 18, 1920. This was when the 19th Amendment to the U.S. Constitution was ratified, or approved. For nearly 150 years before that, only men could vote. It took many years for the suffrage movement to achieve its goal of gaining equal voting rights for women.

One of the major leaders of the movement was Carrie Lane Chapman Catt, who was born in Ripon, Wisconsin, on January 9, 1859. When she was 10 years old, she moved to a farm near Charles City, Iowa, that her father and brother had established. Catt and her mother had to travel by train and wagon to get to the frontier town. The area was so wild that wolves prowled nearby. One night, when she was returning home from a friend's house, she was frightened by one of the animals, but it did not harm her.

Carrie Chapman Catt

Even as a youngster, Catt thought it was important to vote. She always asked why women were denied that right. In her mind, no one had a good answer to this question.

She attended Iowa State College, earning a bachelor of science degree in 1880. After graduation, Catt took a job as principal of Mason City High

In 1920, Wisconsin was one of the first two states to approve the 19th Amendment to the Constitution, which gave women the right to vote. Illinois was the other.

School and went on to be named the area's superintendent of schools in 1883. Many people thought she would not be successful. They believed that only a man could effectively discipline schoolchildren.

But Catt proved them wrong. On the first day in her new job, she took a leather strap and spanked nine boys who disrupted their classes. Her reputation spread as a woman who would not be pushed around.

In 1885, she married Leo Chapman, owner of the *Mason City Republican* newspaper. Always fond of writing, Catt became assistant editor. When her husband died on a business trip a year later, Catt needed to find another job. While looking for work, she observed how many young women often worked in dirty and dangerous conditions. And so for the rest of her career, she sought to improve the safety of the places where women worked.

Catt joined the Iowa Woman Suffrage Association and became one of its principal speakers. She married George William Catt in 1890. She traveled around the country with him in his construction job before settling in New York City. When they married, they agreed that she could spend two months of the year on the road working on behalf of the suffrage movement. Catt's husband was one of the few men at the time who favored allowing women the right to vote.

From 1900 to 1914 and from 1915 to 1920, Catt was president of the National American Woman Suffrage Association. President Woodrow Wilson and other male politicians supported women's suffrage because of the efforts of Catt and her movement to promote it. When the 19th Amendment was approved five years later, she went on to work for worldwide suffrage rights.

Among the many honors she received was an honorary degree from the University of Wyoming, the first state to grant women the right to vote. Catt died in 1947, the same year in which the League of Women Voters set up a foundation to help women learn about the democratic process. ♦

Hamlin Garland (1860–1940)

author

The rugged landscape of northwestern Wisconsin was the setting for many of Hamlin Garland's short stories. He knew this area very well because he was born in West Salem, Wisconsin, on September 14, 1860. This is a small town not far from La Crosse. As a boy in search of adventure, he loved exploring the area's ridges and the river valleys, called coulees. In 1884, he moved to Boston where he earned a living by teaching and writing.

He was interested in science, economics and many other subjects. This curiosity made his writing much better. Garland's fictional characters were always trying to discover something new, just as he was. In 1887, he returned to the Midwest, where he observed the tough life led by small farmers. This experience was the basis for his first book, a collection of short stories called *Main-Traveled Roads*. The volume was published in 1891. It talked about soldiers returning from the Civil War, kids growing up on farms, and the difficulties of day-to-day living on the Wisconsin frontier.

Hamlin Garland

Garland was also active in politics. He campaigned and wrote stories on behalf of many reform candidates. He gave lectures around the country about the hardships of farm life. This activity led to other important books: *Crumbling Idols* (1894) and *Rose of Dutcher's Coolly* (1895).

He visited England in 1899 and met famous authors, playwrights, and business leaders. But Garland was equally at home traveling in the American West. He became an authority on Native Americans, who he believed were to be treated fairly and honestly. This view was expressed in his book *The Captain of the Gray Horse Troop*, which was published in 1902 and became very popular. Garland even wrote about the spiritual world in *The Shadow World*, released in 1908.

His most famous works were *A Son of the Middle Border* (1917) and *A Daughter of the Middle Border* (1921). These tales related the hardships of pioneer life, as settlers struggled to make new lives on the far prairies. Garland won the Pulitzer Prize, a highly respected honor for authors, for *A Daughter of the Middle Border*. Both novels were autobiographical, telling much about the author's own growing-up years.

Garland died on March 4, 1940, at his home in Los Angeles, California. Over his career, he wrote almost 50 novels and story collections. His home in West Salem, Wisconsin, is now a museum and historical site. ◆

Theodora Winton Youmans

(1863–1932)

suffrage leader

For many years, Theodora Winton Youmans was a leading Wisconsin suffragist, who is a supporter of the women's right to vote. She helped win approval of the 19th Amendment to the U.S. Constitution that gave women this right in 1920.

Youmans was born in a log cabin in Assippunion, Wisconsin, on February 1, 1863, and raised in the farm community of Prospect Hill. She died on August 17, 1932. During her life, she accomplished a great deal to advance the cause of women's rights in Wisconsin and the nation.

Theodora Winton Youmans

As a youngster, she spoke both German and English. This was in honor of both her family heritage and the New World where she lived. Youmans became a reporter on the *Waukesha Freeman* newspaper in the 1880s, an unusual job for a young woman of her day. Youmans's hard work earned her the position of assistant editor. Throughout the 1890s, her newspaper stories often played up the importance of women in the home and in the professional world.

One of the most respected women in Wisconsin during the 20th century was Dr. Kate Pelham Newcomb of Minocqua. This brave physician often used snowshoes to reach patients living far off the main roads in northern Wisconsin. For her efforts, she was known as the Angel on Snowshoes.

Wisconsin men, like many around the country at the time, objected strongly to giving women the right to vote. In 1912, they defeated a women's suffrage vote in the state by an huge margin of two to one. Also in 1912, eager to change this situation, the spunky Youmans became president of the Wisconsin Women's Suffrage Association. She was the first Wisconsin-born woman to hold this position.

This group had been formed in 1869 to support women's rights. Two other women had been its president before her. Milwaukee's Laura Ross Wolcott was the state's first woman doctor, and the Reverend Olympia Brown of Racine was one of Wisconsin's first woman ministers. However, neither were state natives. Through her hard work over the next seven years, Youmans molded public opinion in favor of women voting. Her efforts paid off when Congress approved the 19th Amendment in 1920.

But Youmans did not rest after this hard-won race to help women become voters. She also worked tirelessly toward paving the way for the equal rights amendment to Wisconsin's state constitution. It was the nation's first such guarantee of women's equal rights under the law.

Youmans ran for Congress as a Republican in 1924 but lost. It would be another 74 years before a Wisconsin woman would be elected to Congress. In 1999, Madison's Tammy Baldwin took her seat in the United States House of Representatives. Youmans probably would have smiled at the victory. ♦

John R. Ringling (1866–1936)
circus owner and businessman

"**H**old yer hosses! Here come the elephants!"

Generations ago, kids everywhere thrilled to this yell. It meant the circus was in town. And Wisconsin really knew what the circus world was all about. The state was home to dozens of circuses in the 1800s and early 1900s.

The best-known circus family in the world, the Ringling Brothers, got their start in Wisconsin. Their father was a German farmer and the family name was originally Ruengeling. Of the seven Ringling brothers, John led the circus to its greatest heights. He was born on May 3, 1866, in McGregor, Iowa, just across the Mississippi River from Wisconsin. The Ruengeling family moved to Wisconsin shortly afterwards.

The entire family loved the small circuses that toured the state during Wisconsin's frontier days. The lure of the sawdust ring was hard to shake. When John and four of his brothers (Charles, Albert C., Alfred T.,

The five Ringling Brothers; John R. is at the lower right

The Fennimore Doll Museum in the western Wisconsin town of Fennimore has more than 5,000 dolls on display.

and Otto) were young men, they decided to start their own show. They changed their name in the process. Their Classical Concert Company soon grew into the Ringling Brothers Circus. Two other brothers, A.G. and Henry, also worked for the show but were not co-owners.

 John Ringling played a clown in the circus's first productions. His skill at organizing, however, quickly landed him a position as a manager. Ringling became the show's booking agent and then handled its transportation needs.

In 1907, the Ringlings purchased their main rival, the Barnum and Bailey Circus. This made them the largest tent show on the road. Two years later, they put on their first production in New York City's Madison Square Garden, attracting thousands of circus fans for every performance.

All of John's brothers had died by 1930 so he became president of the American Circus Corporation. The company, the largest of its kind in the world, managed the Sells-Floto, the John Robinson, the Sparks, and the Al G. Barnes circuses and the Hagenbeck-Wallace Animal Show. Ringling turned his attention to other business opportunities, as well. He built railroads in Montana and Oklahoma. A town in each state is named Ringling in his honor.

Later, Ringling settled down in Sarasota, Florida. There, he built the John and Mabel Ringling Art Museum to hold his vast art collection valued at more than $20 million. He died on December 2, 1936, in New York City.

From 1884 through the winter of 1917–18, the Ringlings head-quartered their show in Baraboo, a small town along the Baraboo River. Elephants bathing in the river became a familiar sight for the local children. Today, the old barns and offices of the circus house the Circus World Museum, a state historical site that opened in 1959. Many of the wagons displayed there are brought to Milwaukee each year for the Great Circus Parade. ◆

Laura Ingalls Wilder (1867–1957)

author

Laura Ingalls Wilder was born on February 7, 1867, in the village of Pepin, Wisconsin, along the rolling waters of the Mississippi River. Her father and mother were typical pioneers. Searching for the perfect homestead, they lived in Wisconsin, Missouri, Kansas, Iowa, Minnesota, and South Dakota. As the daughter of a pioneer family, Wilder learned how to pluck chickens, sew a quilt, and build a log cabin. She used these and other experiences in writing her first book, *Farmer Boy*. It was published in 1933 when she was age 65, after her daughter encouraged her to write it.

But Wilder actually had a long career as a newspaper writer before attempting novels. She wrote articles about everything from farming to building a house. Yet she is best remembered for her novels.

As a daughter of the prairie and later as the wife of a frontier farmer, Almanzo James Wilder, she endured many hardships. She knew exactly what it meant to face droughts, floods, swarms of grass-hoppers, and the deaths of children. And she had great skill in telling these stories from a young person's point of view. In addition to *Farmer Boy*, her most popular books are *On the Banks of Plum Creek* (1937), *By the Shores of Silver Lake* (1939), *Little House on the Prairie* (1941), *Little Town on the Prairie* (1941), and *Those Happy Golden Years* (1943). Her books have sold 20 million copies in at least 14 languages. They have even been published in Braille, a special language for visually challenged people.

Many of her books were published during the Great Depression. This was a period in the 1930s of great economic hardship. Banks closed, farmers lost their farms, and millions of workers were out of work around the world. Wilder's stories were successful because they told about a family that could make it through hard times on its own.

There are about 78,000 farms in Wisconsin. In 1998, the size of the average farm was about 210 acres, with a land value of around $1,525 per acre.

Wilder won many awards for her clear writing and interesting stories. In 1954, the American Library Association established the Laura Ingalls Wilder Award, given every five years to an author who has made a lasting impact on children's literature. Her works were also the basis for the television series *Little House on the Prairie*, which ran from 1974 to 1982.

Even with all her honors and fame, Wilder kept in close touch with youngsters who wrote her letters. She was always glad to hear from her readers. She listened to their stories.

Laura Ingalls Wilder

She died on February 10, 1957, in Mansfield, Missouri, in a farm house that she and her husband built many years before. Today, there are several museums in other houses where Wilder also lived, including those in Pepin, Wisconsin, and Walnut Grove, Minnesota. These places are so warm and friendly that it seems Wilder herself will appear to give visitors a friendly greeting. ◆

Frank Lloyd Wright (1867–1959)

architect

Frank Lloyd Wright was born on June 8, 1867, in central Wisconsin's Richland Center. Wright's mother, Anna Lloyd-Jones, was from Wales and moved to the United States with her family in 1845. She always hoped her son would be an architect. Before Wright was born, she paged through books filled with pictures of English cathedrals. His father, William Wright, who was born in Westfield, Massachusetts, was a minister and musician.

As a child, Frank Lloyd Wright was always moving to different towns because of his father's work. In his teens, he settled in Madison to attend the University of Wisconsin to study civil engineering. Young Wright was restless there, wanting to be surrounded by great works of architecture. So, after two years, he decided to leave school and head to Chicago, a big city full of great buildings. There must be great architects there, he figured.

Frank Lloyd Wright, shown here with his wife Olgivanna

At first, Wright worked as a draftsman in the engineering office of Adler and Sullivan. This was one of the country's leading architectural firms at the time. He designed and built private homes for some of the company's clients. These homes showed an original and

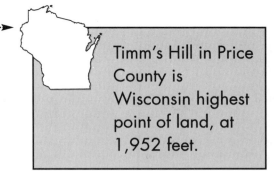

Timm's Hill in Price County is Wisconsin highest point of land, at 1,952 feet.

independent talent that allowed Wright to open his own business. Over the next 20 years, Wright became one of the best-known architects in the United States. His mother would have been proud.

Though Wright died on April 9, 1959, he remains one of the most influential figures in modern Western architecture. Wright's original building style is based on natural forms. He called it "organic architecture." He liked low, sweeping roof lines that hung over walls of windows. But even for master architects, there can be problems. Although they looked good in dry weather, the flat roofs that he favored sometimes leaked when it rained.

Many of Wright's buildings featured huge brick or stone fireplaces located at their center, with surrounding open rooms. His view of architecture was romantic, and his most spectacular buildings were based on the forms and shapes he saw in nature.

One of Wright's most famous designs is that of the S. C. Johnson and Son Wax Company Administration Center in Racine. Monona Terrace, Madison's convention hall completed in 1997, is also based on his plans.

Although he traveled around the world, Wright called Wisconsin his home. Taliesin East, where he built his house, studios, and a school, is in Spring Green. The land was a gift from his mother. Taliesin was nearly destroyed by fire in 1914 and in 1925. He rebuilt it each time, and the buildings still sit in the rolling hills above the Wisconsin River. Visitors enjoy touring the property, a monument to Wright's great creativity and skill. ◆

Harry Houdini (1874–1926)

magician

Harry Houdini was one of the greatest escape artists and magicians of all time. He was born Erich Weiss on April 6, 1874, in Hungary. When he was five years old, he and his family settled in Appleton. His father, Rabbi Samuel Weiss, served at Temple Zion synagogue and was the first rabbi in Outagamie County. After young Erich became a professional magician, he changed his name to Houdini after Jean Houdin, a popular French magician he admired.

Houdini's first job was that of a circus trapeze artist, and so his body needed to be limber in order to perform all the dangerous aerial stunts. He then learned to contort his body into many shapes. Houdini constantly practiced escaping from all sorts of cages, trunks, and boxes. He acted as a consultant to police departments, demonstrating his escape techniques. This helped jails and prisons become more secure. His ability to get away earned him the nickname the King of Handcuffs.

One of his tricks was to be tied up in chains or placed in a straitjacket and dangled upside down high over a river, canyon, or street. And with no net under him! He always wriggled free in seconds. In another stunt, Houdini was bound up in rope and locked in a trunk wrapped in steel tape. His helpers then dropped him into

Harry Houdini

During the 19th century, North Woods lumberjacks spun tall tales about the hodag, a large beast that they said roamed the land. In 1896, Eugene Shepard claimed to have captured one, a hairy monster seven feet long and nearly three feet tall, in the woods near Rhinelander. It turned out that Shepard's beast was made of old animal skins and a metal frame. But the story of the hodag lives on today, and Rhinelander still takes great pride in the legend.

the cold, deep waters of New York City's East River. He freed himself and was out of the water in 59 seconds.

Throughout his career, Houdini worked hard to expose frauds and fakers. He especially did not believe people who claimed they could talk with the dead. These crooks used tricks to convince their listeners that they were in touch with departed loved ones. He showed how the cheaters knocked on the floor or under tables and used other gimmicks to fool their clients.

Houdini's death was as strange as his life. While performing in Montreal, Canada, he was asked by a young student how strong he was. So the magician suggested that the fellow hit him in the stomach to find out. But the man punched Houdini before he could prepare himself for the blow. As a result, the great magician died of a ruptured appendix a few days later, on October 31, 1926. His last words to his brother Theo were, "I'm tired of fighting. I guess this thing is going to get me." Before he died, he was said to have told his wife that he would reappear to her after he was buried. But he never did.

Houdini wrote several books, including *Handcuff Secrets* (1907) and *A Magician among the Spirits* (1924). He also appeared in a couple of silent films. *Houdini*, a 1953 Hollywood movie, was a dramatic account of the magician's life. The Houdini Historical Center in Appleton's Outagamie County Museum has a large exhibit of his handcuffs and leg irons, newspaper clippings, and other memorabilia. If you visit there, you can even try to escape from a pair of cuffs. ♦

Zona Gale (1874–1938)

author

Zona Gale was one of Wisconsin's most popular authors in the 1920s and 1930s. She often wrote about her hometown of Portage, calling it Friendship Village in many of her stories.

Gale was born on August 26, 1874. Even as a little girl, she dreamed of being a writer. She printed her first "book" at age seven and continued writing through high school. After graduating from the University of Wisconsin in 1895, she went on to receive her master's degree in 1899. She then moved to Milwaukee to work for several newspapers. The deadlines she faced there helped her write better. She worked in Milwaukee from 1899 to 1901, before deciding it was time to follow the bright lights of New York.

Zona Gale

Gale became a reporter on the *New York Evening World*. Never wanting to waste a minute or lose a creative idea, she often jotted down notes for short stories while waiting for interviews in city hall or even in police stations. In 1904, she published her first fictional story in the magazine *Success*. In 1905, she returned home to Portage to continue writing fiction full time.

Among her many novels were *Romance Island* (1906), *Heart's Kindred* (1915), *Birth*

The Milwaukee Public Library's Central Branch building holds more than two million books. Among all its branches, the entire Milwaukee system contains more than three million volumes.

(1918), *Miss Lulu Bett* (1920), and *Light Woman* (1937). Her many collections of short stories included *Mothers to Men* (1911), *Peace in Friendship Village* (1919), and *Old-Fashioned Tales* (1933). She turned her novel *Miss Lulu Bett* into a play, which was highly praised by critics. They said the production "heralded the dawn of a mature American drama." The play also won the Pulitzer Prize for drama in 1921.

Gale never seemed to stop composing more plays, poetry, and essays. Her book *Portage, Wisconsin, and Other Essays* (1928) was a collection of reflections about her historically rich hometown. Reviewers said that her books accurately pictured the sights and sounds of rural life. They captured the daily lives of people in small Midwestern communities.

When she was 54 years old, she did slow down enough in 1928 to marry William L. Breese, a Portage businessman.

Gale was also active in social causes. She served on the University of Wisconsin Board of Regents from 1923 to 1929 and on the Wisconsin Free Library Commission from 1923 to 1938. She was an active supporter of reform issues on the state and national levels.

In addition to winning the Pulitzer Prize, Gale was given an honorary doctor of letters degree from the University of Wisconsin. On December 27, 1938, she died of pneumonia in Chicago. Her home in Portage is now a historical site and often serves as a meeting place for writing and library programs. ◆

William "Billy" Mitchell
(1879–1936)

aviator

Military aviator William "Billy" Mitchell was born in France on December 29, 1879. However, his family had strong Wisconsin ties. His grandfather, Alexander Mitchell (whose biography is on pages 18 and 19), was a banker in early Milwaukee and a congressman from Wisconsin. His father, John Mitchell, was a U.S. senator.

After college, young Mitchell joined the army and served in Cuba and the Philippines during the Spanish-American War. He loved flying, having learned the skill from Orville Wright, one of the inventors of the first successful airplane.

Billy Mitchell

During World War I, Mitchell became commander of the U.S. Air Service, a branch of the army. He saw many opportunities for the use of airplanes in war. Mitchell even suggested that soldiers be parachuted behind enemy lines. However, his commanders would not let him try this novel idea and others that he had.

That did not stop Mitchell. Even after the war, he urged his superiors to invest in a strong air force separate from the army. But many people in the 1920s, including President Warren G.

The airport in Milwaukee named after General Billy Mitchell is the largest in Wisconsin. More than 400 commercial flights to and from 90 major cities are provided daily by 20 airlines. Each year, more than 5.5 million passengers use the airport, and there are 210,000 takeoffs and landings. If all its concrete and asphalt surfaces were combined into a single roadway, it would stretch 143 miles.

Harding, did not agree. This angered Mitchell. To show what air power could do, he received approval for his pilots to bomb and sink two old ships. The president watched the display but did not change his mind.

Mitchell kept trying to get support for a strong air force. He was also concerned about the growing power of Japan. Still, the government did not pay attention. Mitchell was demoted, or lowered in rank, from brigadier general to colonel. But the flier would not be quiet. When the dirigible *Shenandoah*, a giant steerable balloon, crashed in the mid-1920s, 14 crew members were killed. Mitchell blamed the army for the accident.

His outspoken views resulted in Mitchell's court martial in 1926, a military trial in which he was suspended from the army. But before he could be punished, Mitchell resigned. As a civilian, he kept up his attack on army officials and continued to push for a more powerful air force. Fighting to the end, Mitchell died on February 19, 1936.

Mitchell's warnings about Japan came true when that country attacked Pearl Harbor on December 7, 1941. The army finally realized its mistake in ignoring Mitchell's warnings, but it was almost too late.

Mitchell's good reputation was finally restored. In 1942, even though he been dead for six years, he was given the rank of major general. The rugged Mitchell bomber, the B-25, was named after him. Mitchell was also awarded the Medal of Honor, which was given to his family in 1948.

A 1955 movie, *The Court-Martial of Billy Mitchell*, was filmed about his life, starring Gary Cooper in the title role. In addition, General Mitchell International Airport in Milwaukee is named in honor of the famous flier who was not afraid to speak his views. ♦

Douglas MacArthur (1880–1964)

soldier

Douglas MacArthur, who led U.S. forces against Japan in World War II, was first and foremost a soldier. This five-star general came from a long line of military men and government servants. His father was a decorated infantry officer in the Civil War. His grandfather was Wisconsin's lieutenant governor and served as governor for a brief time in 1856. MacArthur's brother was a navy captain, serving in the Spanish-American War.

MacArthur was born on January 26, 1880, in Little Rock, Arkansas. He moved to Milwaukee in 1898 from the Philippines, where his father had been commander of United States troops. While in the city, the MacArthurs lived in the Plankinton House, a downtown hotel. MacArthur attended classes at West Division High School before going on to attend the United States Military Academy at West Point.

After graduating in 1903, MacArthur entered the Army Corps of Engineers. He served as an officer during World War I. He was an effective and colorful leader, earning several decorations.

After the war, MacArthur was named superintendent of the military academy and promoted to brigadier general. His reforms there improved its academic standards. He moved on to command U.S. troops in the Philippine Islands. In 1925, he became the youngest person in U.S. Army history to achieve the rank of major general up to that time.

At about the same time, MacArthur served at the court martial of General Billy Mitchell, a noted flier with Wisconsin ties. (Mitchell's biography is on page 48.) President Herbert Hoover appointed MacArthur army chief of staff in 1930. Although the army was small, MacArthur helped bring it up to date and gathered support for a separate air corps, exactly what Mitchell had wanted to do earlier.

MacArthur was a tough soldier who always did his job. In 1932, during the Great Depression, thousands of jobless ex-soldiers marched

Of all the ethnic groups in Wisconsin, people of Philippine ancestry have the highest annual household income, averaging $60,000. The state average is $35,000 per year.

on the U.S. Capitol to demand their pensions. Under orders from President Herbert Hoover, MacArthur had them removed by force. Many people objected to this attack against citizens who had served their country. MacArthur thought that he was doing the only thing a good soldier should do—carry out orders.

When World War II broke out, MacArthur served again in the Philippines. He was ordered home just before his outnumbered forces were overwhelmed and captured by the Japanese. His famous words upon departing were, "I shall return." And four years later he did. But it took American forces many bitter battles on Pacific islands before he made it back. He presided over Japan's surrender in ceremonies on September 2, 1945.

MacArthur then was named to oversee the political and economic recovery of Japan. When the Korean War broke out in 1950, MacArthur headed the United Nations troops. But he loudly disagreed with President Harry Truman's policies and was relieved of his command. Yet he was welcomed as a hero when he returned to the United States, including a visit to Milwaukee in April 1951.

After MacArthur retired from the army, he became a business executive. He died on April 5, 1964. MacArthur Square in downtown Milwaukee is named after him. ♦

Douglas MacArthur

William Harley (1880–1943)
& Arthur Davidson (1881–1950)
businessmen

The name Harley-Davidson means one thing: Motorcycles . . . powerful motorcycles.

Founders of one of the world's most popular motorcycle manufacturing companies, William S. Harley and Arthur D. Davidson were boyhood friends in Milwaukee. When they were in their twenties, Harley was a draftsman and Davidson was a pattern maker in a local manufacturing company. Since they loved bicycles, they decided to make a motorized cycle. A coworker inspired them by showing them plans for an engine he had seen in a French factory where he once had worked.

As a result, around 1901, the two men began tinkering with their invention. They needed help so they encouraged Davidson's brothers, William A. and Walter, to join them. This was an excellent decision because both were fine machinists. At first, the four worked in a basement. But they soon had to move into a friend's larger workshop, one that had a drill press and other heavy equipment. Soon, they needed even more room. In 1903, the Davidsons convinced their father, a Scottish-born cabinetmaker, to build their first "factory." This

Arthur Davidson (left); William Harley (right)

52

Wisconsin's first "highway" to cut across the state ran from Green Bay to Prairie du Chien in the southwest part of the state. At first, only a dirt track known as the Old Military Road, the trail was built in the 1830s. It was used for transporting supplies and troops to military outposts along the way.

was merely a shed in the elder Davidson's backyard. On the door, he painted "Harley-Davidson Motor Company."

In their spare time that first year, the young men made three motorcycles. By the next year, they produced eight machines. The following year, they enlarged their operations even more. By then, most of their father's backyard was used up. Soon, there was no room at all.

The young Davidsons turned to an uncle in Madison for help. He arranged for them to buy land in Milwaukee, where they could construct a real factory. By 1906, Harley and the three Davidsons had quit their regular jobs to focus on the growing company.

From then on, Harley-Davidson Motor Company blossomed. By 1909, the company's 35 employees had produced 1,000 machines. In 1910, the firm moved into a concrete building that could hold 149 workers. They made 3,200 motorcycles that year and worked on engine designs that were perfected over the years.

William Harley, the company's chief engineer and treasurer, was born on December 29, 1880, and died on September 18, 1943. Arthur Davidson, secretary and general manager, was born in 1881 and died on December 30, 1950. His two brothers died in 1937 and 1942.

Family members have remained involved with the Harley-Davidson firm over the years. At the end of the twentieth century, these include "Willie" G. Davidson, grandson of William A., who is vice president of styling. Willie's son, William J. Davidson, is in charge of product development.

A lot of competitors have followed in the Harley-Davidson footsteps but many have failed. By the late 1990s, Harley-Davidson was the world's top producer of heavyweight motorcycles, employing 6,200 workers worldwide and making about 185,000 cycles each year. ♦

Edna Ferber (1885–1968)

journalist and author

Edna Jessica Ferber had a keen eye for detail and knew how to dig for facts. As a young girl, she always asked questions. She wanted to know how things worked and why people acted the way they did. Her parents, Jacob and Julia Ferber, were very patient and answered as many questions as they could. Not surprisingly, she also wanted to write stories and decided at an early age that working for a newspaper would be a great career.

Ferber was born on August 15, 1885, in Kalamazoo, Michigan. She moved with her parents to Iowa before coming to Appleton, Wisconsin, in 1897. There, she graduated from high school and got her first job at the local newspaper, the *Appleton Crescent*. At age 17, she was doing exactly what she always wanted to do: write and find answers. She was an excellent reporter and soon moved on to the *Milwaukee Journal* in the early 1900s. Ferber became a police reporter, one of the toughest jobs on the paper. She worked very hard but became sick and had to return home in 1905.

Edna Ferber

While recovering, she wrote some short stories and her first novel, *Dawn O'Hara*, about a woman newspaper reporter in Milwaukee. This, she thought, was even better than chasing

The five largest ethnic groups in Wisconsin are the Germans, with 2,209,701 people; the Polish, with 325,320; the Irish, with 281,309; the Norwegians, with 257,345; and African-Americans, with 244,305.

around the Milwaukee County Courthouse looking for news. Her second novel, *Fanny Herself*, told of a young Jewish girl growing up in a town much like Appleton. Much of the story was taken from incidents in Ferber's own life. After a time, she moved to New York City and continued her writing, winning the Pulitzer Prize in 1925 for her novel *So Big*. The Pulitzer is one of the most important literary honors in the country.

Her novel about a floating theater, *Show Boat*, was made into a Broadway musical, three films, and a radio series after it was published in 1926. When Ferber was writing the story, she moved to North Carolina for a few months to live and work on a riverboat. She wanted to get the details right.

Ferber always did an excellent job of describing people. This was one of her strongest writing talents. She wrote about Polish tobacco farmers in Connecticut, pioneers in Oklahoma, Texas gamblers, and Wisconsin loggers. She was always interested in theater and sometimes thought about becoming an actress. Although she never performed on stage, Ferber wrote several plays that became great hits.

This talented author was proud to have grown up in Wisconsin and liked to write about the Midwest. She was popular because her readers could identify with her characters, and they had the same challenges in their lives. "I really am one of them," she said.

Ferber died on April 16, 1968, in New York City. ◆

Georgia O'Keefe (1887–1986)

artist

From her growing-up years on the plains of south-central Wisconsin, Georgia O'Keefe carried her love of nature and the wide outdoors to many exotic places. But her favorite scenes to paint were the mountains and deserts of the southwestern United States. There she could depict brilliant landscapes of sunny mesas and plateaus. Her keen eye helped her show the strange whiteness of bleached buffalo skulls. The vivid colors of exotic flowers also attracted her attention.

O'Keefe's ability to capture the light and color of her subjects earned her a faithful following of collectors. Today, many of her paintings are worth tens of thousands of dollars. Some have been valued at more than $100,000.

Georgia O'Keefe

She was born on November 15, 1887, in Sun Prairie, Wisconsin, a village a few miles east of Madison. By the time she was 13, she knew she wanted to be an artist. In 1904, she enrolled in the Art Institute of Chicago and went on for further studies at the Art Students League in New York City. Lacking financial help from home, young O'Keefe had to support herself as an advertising illustrator and art teacher.

While in New York, she met the dashing photographer

There are 24,244 Milwaukeeans of Mexican ancestry, out of a population of 59,903 in the state. Fiesta Mexican is one of the city's largest ethnic festivals, held each summer at the Henry W. Maier Lakefront Festival Park (Summerfest grounds). Mexican rodeos are also held regularly at the Racine County Fairgrounds in Union Grove. Many of the first Mexican families arrived in Wisconsin in the 1920s. The Hispanic Chamber of Commerce is a major business organization in Wisconsin.

Alfred Stieglitz. He was already famous on the art circuit and made sure that her paintings were displayed in his well-known Gallery 291. They fell in love and were married in 1924.

At first, O'Keefe emphasized abstract painting, which uses new and strange images to communicate ideas and emotions. She began painting objects from odd angles and different perspectives. Challenging her viewers to think deeply about what they were seeing was always one of her strengths. She and Stieglitz visited New Mexico in 1929 and fell in love with the wild countryside. O'Keefe returned to the area every summer for the next 17 years to paint.

After Stieglitz died in 1946, she moved permanently to New Mexico. She was attracted by the desert and what she saw as its many symbols of life and death.

In 1970, O'Keefe received a Gold Medal from the National Institute of Arts and Letters. She was given the Medal of Freedom in 1977, one of the country's highest awards for personal achievement. Toward the end of her life, O'Keefe's eyesight began to fail but she continued to paint as much as possible, despite not being able to see as clearly as before.

She died on March 6, 1986, in Santa Fe, New Mexico. A roadside marker in Sun Prairie points out the farm where O'Keefe was born and spent her childhood days. ♦

Aldo Leopold (1887–1948)

environmentalist

By the time Aldo Leopold was 11 years old, he had drawn pictures of 39 bird species in his journal. This was the start of his deep interest in the environment. Over his career, he was a forester, game manager, scientist, and writer. He received many honors for promoting his great passion for nature.

Rand Aldo Leopold was born in Burlington, Iowa, on January 11, 1887. The fields and forests around Burlington offered the young boy plenty of opportunities to appreciate wildlife. Leopold recalled that his sister Marie "was always out climbing around the bluffs, or going down to the river, or going across the river into the woods." He was always close behind.

Aldo Leopold

His parents—especially his father, Carl—developed a great love for the outdoors in their four children. Even in winter, Aldo, Marie, Carl Jr., and Frederic would be taken to the woods to learn about plants and insects. They learned to recognize animal dens and their tracks. Leopold's passion for wildlife grew with him. This went hand in hand with his very special writing skills.

He studied forestry at Yale University, where he was graduated in 1908. The

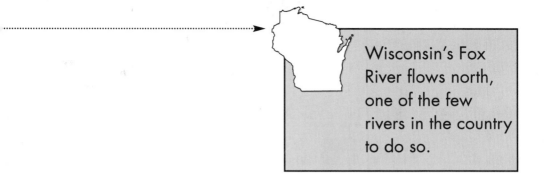

Wisconsin's Fox River flows north, one of the few rivers in the country to do so.

following year, he started working for the United States Forest Service. By 1912, he had reached the rank of supervisor.

Leopold was a very good scholar. In 1933, he became professor of wildlife management at the University of Wisconsin in Madison. He also had a great desire to put theories into practice. So, in 1935, he and his family purchased an abandoned farm near Baraboo in central Wisconsin. Because of the sandy soil, it was hard to grow crops on this sprawling and dry stretch of flat, open land. But Leopold was convinced he could make that earth fertile through strong conservation efforts.

In one of his most famous books, *A Sand County Almanac*, he recorded his experiences on the farm that had become his favorite place to live. There, Leopold and his wife, Estella, raised their five children. The youngsters were taught how to appreciate and enjoy all the natural things around them.

In 1934, President Franklin Roosevelt appointed Leopold a member of the Special Commission on Wildlife Restoration. For his accomplishments, he was awarded a medal by the Permanent Wildlife Protection Fund and by *Outdoor Life* magazine.

Leopold died of heart attack on April 21, 1948, after a heroic attempt to save a neighbor's farm from a fire. ◆

Alfred Lunt (1892–1977)
& Lynn Fontanne (1887–1983)

actors

From the 1920s through the 1950s, Alfred Lunt and his wife, Lynn Fontanne, were the most famous acting couple in America. Everywhere they performed, the two thrilled audiences with their charm, creativity, wit, and skill.

Born in Milwaukee on August 19, 1892, Lunt attended Carroll College in Waukesha before being drawn to the theater. Lynn Fontanne was born on December 6, 1887, in London, England. They were married in 1922 and regularly performed together. The couple appeared often in New York's Broadway district, where a theater is now named in their honor. England was also a regular stop on their around-the-world tours, always a homecoming visit for Fontanne.

Alfred Lunt and Lynn Fontanne

Lunt and Fontanne studied people around them to learn more about human behavior. This careful observation helped them in their acting roles. They costarred in 27 major plays, including *The Doctor's Dilemma* (1927), *Design for Living* (1933), *The Taming of the Shrew* (1935), *Idiot's Delight* (1936), *The Seagull* (1938), and *The Visit* (1958). They starred in one movie, *The Guardsman*, in 1931. The couple

The Milwaukee Repertory and the First Stage theater companies in Milwaukee have outreach programs for young actors.

appeared on numerous television shows and won an Emmy award for their roles in *The Magnificent Yankee* (1965).

But Lunt was never far from his Wisconsin roots. He and Fontanne built a home on 120 acres near Genesee Depot, a village in Waukesha County. Named Ten Chimneys, the estate was always a work in progress, with additions and changes constantly underway. Their home grew from a four-level main house to a group of buildings that included guest houses, a swimming pool, a greenhouse, and other structures. The site has been remodeled and is now a museum.

When Lunt and Fontanne lived there, they operated a small farm. Since Lunt was a trained chef, he always fixed wonderful meals using fresh ingredients. He usually fed the carpenters, electricians, and other workmen at Ten Chimneys. Early in the day, their food orders were taken. Around noon, a waiter in a white jacket served them lunch on a silver tray!

Many famous actors, playwrights, and musicians dropped by to relax. Among them were Helen Hayes, Carol Channing, Katharine Hepburn, Laurence Olivier, Robert Sherwood, and Noel Coward.

Lunt died on August 2, 1977, in Chicago. His wife died on July 30, 1983 in Genesee Depot. They are both buried in Milwaukee's Forest Home Cemetery.

In 1999, the United States Postal Service issued a stamp in their honor. ♦

Thornton Wilder (1897–1975)

author

Thornton Wilder wrote about how people relate to each other in many different ways. One of his most famous novels is *The Bridge of San Luis Rey*. The compelling story tells how five individuals die when a bridge falls into a mountain gorge in Peru in 1712. Instead of being sad, his tale weaves together each of the victims' lives. In his classic play *Our Town*, Wilder uses a young man and woman as the central figures. He places them in a small town, showing how their love affects those around them. Often produced in schools, the play has remained popular for many years because of its message of caring and affection.

Some critics have said that Wilder was like a sculptor, turning words over in his mind like the artist chips at a stone. He always respected his characters and made their inner thoughts seem real.

Thornton Wilder

Wilder was born on April 17, 1897, in Madison, Wisconsin. But he spent part of his early years in China, where his father worked for the State Department as a consular official. Wilder enjoyed being a student, attending several universities in the United States and the American Academy in Rome. Although he was a peaceful man, he served in the coast artillery in World War I and in military intelligence in

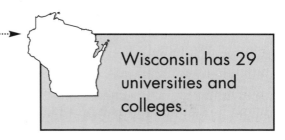

World War II. He earned many honors for his hard work on behalf of the country. Wilder also enjoyed teaching at universities in Hawaii and Chicago, as well as at Harvard.

Wilder always wanted to be an author, writing his first novel, *The Cabala*, in 1926. But it was *The Bridge of San Luis Rey*, published in 1927, that made him a success. The book won a Pulitzer Prize, one of our nation's highest honors for a literary work. Since it was a best seller, it gave him the financial freedom to write five more novels and many plays.

Our Town won him another Pulitzer Prize in 1938. This made him the first writer to be awarded a Pulitzer in both fiction and drama. And Wilder was not done yet. He won a third Pulitzer for his comedy *The Skin of Our Teeth*, which was released in 1942.

Noted for their humor and satire, some of Wilder's works have gone through several changes in form, including being made into plays and movies. His story "The Merchant of Yonkers," written in 1939, was turned into a play, *The Matchmaker*, in 1955. It finally was made into the award-winning Broadway musical *Hello, Dolly!*

Wilder has often been considered one of the most important play-wrights in the United States. He died at home on December 7, 1975. ◆

Golda Meir (1898–1978)

world leader

Golda Meir was always proud of her Jewish heritage. She also loved her homeland of Palestine. This love took her from her girlhood in Milwaukee to that far-off land in the Middle East, years before it became the nation of Israel. Meir later became prime minister of Israel, one of the first women to reach such a powerful position in any country.

Meir was born the daughter of Moshe and Bluma Mabovitch on May 3, 1898, in Ukraine, a region that was part of Russia. In 1906, the family immigrated to Milwaukee, where she attended the Fourth Street School. She then went to North Division High School, graduating in 1912. From there, Meir moved on to the Milwaukee Teachers College, getting her degree in 1917. Golda married Morris Myerson the same year. Later in her life, she changed her name to Meir.

For several years, Meir taught in Milwaukee but always believed that the Jews could reclaim their land in the Middle East. As a young woman, she became active in the Labor Zionist Party. This was a political organization that supported such a home-land. In 1921, she left for Palestine and joined a kibbutz, a farm in the desert where she was put in charge of a chicken-

Golda Meir

raising business. But that was not enough for the always active Meir. She moved to fast-growing Tel Aviv and got a job in the Office of Public Works. During the 1930s and 1940s, she became active in the international Zionist movement. The Zionists encouraged Jews from all over the world to move to Palestine, which was governed by the British at the time.

Those were troubled days in the Middle East, which saw wars, revolutions, and riots. After World War II, the British did not want to give up their control of Palestine and tried to prevent additional Jews from settling there. They sent their navy to blockade the coast. But Meir and other Zionists helped smuggle refugees into the country. This was very dangerous.

Israel finally became a country on May 14, 1948. Meir was one of the signers of its declaration of independence. She went to Russia to represent the interests of Jews in that country and did so well that she was elected to the Israeli Parliament. She was then appointed minister of labor and social insurance. Meir put together a plan to build thousands of houses and apartments for new Jewish settlers.

There was always much to do. She served as Israel's foreign minister from 1956 to 1966 and became the country's fourth prime minister in 1969. She resigned in 1974 after accepting the blame for Israel not being prepared for an attack by its Arab neighbors. Israel did beat them back, but Meir felt it was time for her to retire.

Her autobiography, *My Life*, traced the development of Israel as a modern state. She visited Milwaukee several times, where the Golda Meir School and the library at the University of Wisconsin-Milwaukee are named after her.

Meir died on December 8, 1978. ♦

Spencer Tracy (1900–1967)

actor

Born in Milwaukee on April 5, 1900, Spencer Tracy was one of the country's most popular film actors from the 1940s through the 1970s. He dropped out of high school to enter the navy during World War I. After the war, he finished high school at Northwestern Military and Naval Academy in Lake Geneva, Wisconsin.

He attended Ripon College from 1920 to 1922. At first, Tracy wanted to be a doctor. But when he joined the debate team, one of his teachers was impressed with his ability to learn lines and suggested that he become an actor. He then got the lead in a play and found that he loved the stage. His teacher wrote a letter recommending Tracy to the American Academy of Dramatic Arts in New York City.

Spencer Tracy

When the debate team went to New York, Tracy auditioned at the academy. He was immediately accepted. Tracy was an excellent student, who worked hard at his craft. In the early 1920s, he landed his first Broadway role as a robot in the play *R.U.R.* But times were tough and Tracy had to work at odd jobs while seeking other acting roles. He finally appeared in *The Last Mile*, a play about gangsters. His strong image on stage attracted the attention of the famous film

> The Quadracci Powerhouse Theater, the home of the Milwaukee Repertory acting company, was built as a steam-generating plant in 1900. In 1984, the Wisconsin Electric Power Company donated the structure to the theater company. It took two years to remodel the building. The first performance there was *The Matchmaker*, by Wisconsin-born playwright Thornton Wilder.

director John Ford, who immediately cast him as another gangster in *Up the River*. Tracy was on his way.

In his first films in the early 1930s, Tracy always played the bad guy. But he soon moved into other roles. His rugged good looks, charming smile, and twinkling eyes were better suited for dramatic and comedy roles than for those needing a tough guy image. His big break came in 1935 when he switched from Fox Studios to MGM. He then was given roles that showed how creative he could be.

He was nominated nine times for an Academy Award, the greatest honor given to film performers in this country. Tracy was also the only actor ever to receive Oscar awards two years in a row. He won for the adventure tale *Captains Courageous* in 1937 and *Boys' Town* in 1938.

Although Tracy performed with many famous screen actors, he regularly costarred with the great Katharine Hepburn. They appeared in nine films together, many of which were light-hearted comedies that showed their deep affection for each other.

They were together for Tracy's final movie, *Guess Who's Coming to Dinner*, which was made in 1967. The story dealt with a white couple whose daughter was about to marry an African-American doctor. Tracy received his final Oscar nomination for this part. He died on June 10, 1967, in Beverly Hills, California. ♦

Joseph McCarthy (1908–1957)

senator

Joseph McCarthy was a United States senator from Wisconsin who led a campaign against United States citizens he thought were followers of Communism. During public hearings in the 1950s, he attacked many politicians, military personnel, artists, authors, and scientists. He abused this power so much that he was censured, or publicly condemned, by other senators.

As a result, the McCarthy Era is considered one of the darkest blots on civil liberties in American history. McCarthy was so powerful that many people lost their jobs and reputations by refusing to answer his questions about their politics. Others, whether out of fear or what they thought was patriotism, named their friends and relatives as members of the Communist Party and other such groups.

All this trouble happened right after World War II. At the time, the United States was at odds with the former Soviet Union in what was called the "Cold War." Many people were afraid that the Soviet Union was going to attack the United States. They worried that spies and traitors were already active in this country.

McCarthy graduated from Marquette University and became a lawyer in 1935. Eager

Joseph McCarthy

Bernard Cigrand, a teacher in Waukesha, started Flag Day on June 14, 1885. He was only 19 years old at the time. Many schools around the country still celebrate the holiday.

to enter politics, he was elected to the Tenth Judicial Court of Wisconsin in 1939. When World War II broke out, McCarthy joined the Marine Corps and became an intelligence officer in the South Pacific in the fight against the Japanese. He then ran for the U.S. Senate twice, losing the nomination the first time he tried. He was successful in 1946, defeating Robert M. La Follette Jr. in the Republican primary election.

The new Wisconsin senator kept a low profile until 1950, when he started accusing numbers of people of being Communists. He claimed that many of them worked in the U.S. State Department. He even attacked George Marshall, a former army general, secretary of state, and Nobel Peace Prize winner.

McCarthy was reelected to the Senate in 1952, even though many people wanted to see him defeated. He objected to some of President Dwight D. Eisenhower's appointments and started an investigation into the Army Signal Corps. His fight continued into 1954 when he televised his hearings, claiming there were disloyal officers in the army. The country was shocked and amazed to watch McCarthy's wild antics, and he began to lose popular support.

This was enough for the Senate. As a result of negative stories about McCarthy's finances in some Wisconsin newspapers, the senators condemned him by a vote of 67 to 22 in 1954. With all this weighing on him, McCarthy's influence disappeared. He was almost totally ignored for the rest of his term.

McCarthy was born on November 14, 1908, in Grand Chute, Wisconsin, and died after a long illness on May 2, 1957, in Bethesda, Maryland. ♦

John Bardeen (1908–1991)

scientist

Wisconsin native John Bardeen was the only person to win two Nobel Prizes in physics. The Nobel Prize is one of the world's most important awards given to scientists and other creative people. To win two of these awards in a single career is truly amazing!

In 1956, Bardeen won the prize for inventing the transistor. In 1972, he won again for working on the theory of superconductivity, the ability of some types of metal to conduct electrical currents at very low temperatures.

Bardeen was born on May 23, 1908, in Madison, Wisconsin. His father, Charles, was the first dean of the University of Wisconsin Medical School. So young Bardeen was exposed to the scientific world at an early age. Always interested in mathematics and science, he attended high school in Madison and graduated from the University of Wisconsin in 1928. He received his master's degree from there a year later.

At first, Bardeen worked as a geophysicist for a company in Pennsylvania. But he decided he wanted to do research rather than make a career in industry. So he went back to school to get his doctorate. From 1933 to 1936, he attended Princeton University and took courses at

John Bardeen

The University of
Wisconsin has
more than 40,000
students enrolled at its
Madison campus.

Harvard. After getting his degree in physics and mathematics, he taught at the University of Minnesota. During World War II, he was chief physicist at the Naval Ordnance Laboratory.

After the war, Bardeen joined Bell Laboratories in New Jersey, where he did research in semiconductors. Bardeen and his team were seeking a device that would replace fragile vacuum tubes, which up to that time had been used to direct electric current.

Their research led to what they called the "transfer resistor," or "transistor." This device was smaller, easier to use, and stronger than a vacuum tube. The discovery opened up a new world of electronic wonders. From Bardeen's research, radios, calculators, and computers became faster, smaller, and more efficient. For this work, Bardeen and his coworkers won the Nobel Prize.

Bardeen then became a professor of electrical engineering at the University of Illinois. He developed the BCS theory of super-conductivity, which allowed computers to work even faster. BCS stands for the first letter of Bardeen's name and of the last names of two others who worked on the project, Leon N. Cooper and John R. Schrieffer. The three men shared a Nobel Prize for that work.

Bardeen died on January 30, 1991, in Boston. ◆

Vince Lombardi (1913–1970)

football coach

Anyone who is a Green Bay Packer fan easily recognizes the gap-toothed grin of Vince Lombardi, the team's most famous coach. When you mention his name in Wisconsin, people immediately think of football success.

Lombardi talked tough and acted tough. Between 1959 and 1967, he pushed his players to win, win, win. Under his control, the Packers won six Western Conference championships, five National Football League (NFL) titles, and Super Bowl championships in 1966 and 1967. After retiring from the Packers as its general manager, he took his coaching skills to the Washington Redskins in 1969. He led them to their first winning season in 14 years.

Vince Lombardi

Lombardi's career record was 96 wins, 34 losses, and 6 ties during the regular NFL season. He did just as well in postseason play, with 10 wins, 2 losses, and no ties.

For all his hard work and success, the NFL Hall of Fame awarded him the Distinguished American Award in 1970. The following year, Lombardi was made a member of the Hall of Fame itself.

Born Thomas Vincent Lombardi on June 11, 1913, he was the son of Italian

The Green Bay Packers have won the National Football League title 11 times and the Super Bowl 3 times. The Packers are the only team in the league that is publicly owned. Green Bay is also the smallest city in the country to have an NFL team.

immigrants. His dad was a butcher who supported his son's athletic efforts through high school in Brooklyn, New York, and in college. The young Lombardi was a star player and earned a scholarship to play football at Fordham University in New York City. He was known as a scrappy player. He once caught an opponent's elbow in the mouth, an injury that took 30 stitches to close! That did not slow him down, however. In addition, he did well in the classroom. Even while playing ball, he managed to graduate near the top of his class and make the dean's list every year.

After graduating, Lombardi went to law school at night and worked as an insurance investigator during the day. He still found time to play minor league football on weekends. From 1939 to 1946, he taught science and coached football at St. Cecilia High School in Englewood, New Jersey. While there, his teams won 36 straight games and took six state championships. From high school, he moved up to be a successful assistant coach at the United States Military Academy.

Lombardi switched to coaching pro football in 1954, starting with the New York Giants. He helped the team win numerous NFL titles. In 1959, he was named head coach of the Packers, who had gone 11 years without a winning season. Lombardi quickly changed that. His players, such as Bart Starr and Paul Horning, became some of the best athletes in the league.

Lombardi's coaching style was simple. "Football is two things," he said, "blocking and tackling." His advice worked, as shown by the many victories the Packers racked up. Lombardi died of cancer on September 3, 1970, at Georgetown University Hospital in Washington, D.C. ♦

Woody Herman (1913–1987)

musician

Few bandleaders have had such a long-lasting influence on music as did Woodrow Charles Thomas Herman, better known as Woody. He was born in Milwaukee on May 16, 1913. Herman knew he wanted to be a jazz musician by the time he was eight years old. In the 1920s, he performed in a children's group that played in movie theaters showing silent films. He took music and dance lessons, encouraged by his family and teachers who recognized his talent.

Herman soon began playing in jazz bands. As a teenager, he toured with those led by the famous Tom Gerun, Harry Sosnick, and Gus Arnheim. While on the road, he picked up the sharp, snappy sound on the saxophone and clarinet that became his musical trademarks. In 1934, he joined the Isham Jones Orchestra and fine-tuned his singing.

Striking out on his own, Herman and several friends formed the Band That Plays the Blues in 1936, which was a hit wherever it played. *Woodchopper's Ball*, one of the songs he wrote with the group, has sold five million copies.

Herman went on to organize several other bands, using the country's top musicians. He started many young performers on their

Woody Herman

careers. Saxophone players Stan Getz and Flip Phillips, pianists Ralph Burns and Jimmy Rowles were among them. Herman was quiet and rather shy, always letting his musicians take the limelight. This was unlike some other bandleaders, who wanted to be the stars of the show.

He called each of his next several bands the Herd. They were very popular during World War II, when they entertained troops in stage shows and on the radio. After the war, the Herd I, the Second Herd, the Herd III, and the Thundering Herd kept up with all the latest trends in jazz. Herman even introduced bits of rock and roll into his upbeat sound.

But with his successes, Herman had troubles. He hired a manager who mishandled his money. He was shocked to learn that he owed the government more than a million dollars in taxes. It took the rest of Herman's life to pay off the debt. In 1997, he was seriously injured in an automobile accident, and his wife died of cancer soon after that.

Yet even with all these challenges, Herman never gave up. He earned many awards for his music and celebrated his 50th year in show business with a concert in the Paramount Theater in New York City. Three thousand people attended the program on July 16, 1987. The University of Houston in Texas established the Woody Herman Music Archives at its school of music.

Herman died of heart failure on October 29, 1987, in Los Angeles, California. A giant memorial reunion in 1993 brought together members of his various bands from over the years. Herman fans from around the world attended the concert in Newport Beach, California. ◆

Orson Wells (1915–1985)
actor and director

Film fans say that Orson Wells was one of the best directors that the American movie world ever produced. He is probably best known for his controversial movie *Citizen Kane*, a story about a powerful newspaper publisher. Wells was also a noted radio producer and is always remembered for his scary radio broadcast "The War of the Worlds." Using fake news reports, the program described aliens from Mars attacking the Earth. The show was so real that many people fled their homes in panic.

Wells was born on May 6, 1915, in Kenosha, Wisconsin. He was one of two sons of Richard Wells, an inventor. His mother, Beatrice, was a fine amateur pianist. His parents died when Wells was very young so he

Orson Wells

went to live with a family friend in Chicago. His guardian, Dr. Maurice Bernstein, introduced the young Wells to the active arts scene there. He learned to play the violin, paint, and even perform magic tricks.

When he was 10 years old, Wells went to the Todd School in Woodstock, Illinois, where he fell in love with the theater. He directed several plays and appeared in a student movie. This amazing young man even wrote several textbooks about staging Shakespeare's plays. His suggestions were used in high-school drama classes around the country.

Wells traveled to Ireland when he was 16. He ran out of money there and applied for a job at the Gate Theater in Dublin. He tried to appear older than he was by smoking a cigar and saying he worked in the New York theater. The managers, of course, did not believe him. But they recognized his acting talent. He was hired, making his stage debut in November, 1931.

Upon his return to the United States after a year or so, Wells kept busy with several theater companies. He founded New York's famous Mercury Theater Company when he was only 23 years old. He became well known as a radio actor, appearing in at least a thousand shows over his career. Wells's deep voice thrilled radio audiences listening to *The Shadow*. This was a program about a detective who could become invisible. The Shadow's best-known line was, "Who knows what evil lurks in the heart of men?"

In 1939, Wells signed a contract with RKO Pictures in Hollywood. The deal gave him the opportunity to write, direct, star, and produce his own movies. Only a few people ever had such a great chance to be so creative. Wells went on to pioneer the use of many film techniques that became common in the industry.

Wells died of a heart attack on October 9, 1985. He was in his Hollywood home writing a film script when he died. He is buried in Spain, a long way from his Kenosha boyhood home. ◆

Gaylord Nelson (b. 1916)
politician and environmentalist

Gaylord Nelson was born on June 4, 1916, in the village of Clear Lake, Wisconsin. He was one of 12 children. All the kids in town enjoyed the three lakes in the area, where they fished and swam in the summer and skated in the winter. Nelson was fond of watching the turtles and birds that lived in the surrounding marshes.

Throughout school, Nelson was always interested in politics. He did not like to sit around but always wanted to get things done. After college, he attended the University of Wisconsin Law School and earned his law degree in 1942. Nelson served in the army during World War II, returning to Wisconsin after the war to become active in the Democratic Party.

He decided to run for the Wisconsin State Legislature and was elected senator, holding that position from 1949 to 1958. He was encouraged to run for higher office and figured he would try for governor. Everyone thought the race would be an uphill fight because the Republicans had held that office for years. But Nelson surprised everyone in 1958 with his strong showing at the polls. He earned 53.6% of the votes that were cast. He was a very active governor. One of his proudest moments came when he pushed through a tax on cigarettes. The money was then used to buy wetlands and parks to protect them from development.

After his one term as governor of Wisconsin, Nelson decided to try for another office. He was elected to the U.S. Senate in 1962, a position he held until 1980. In those days, not many people gave much thought to the environment, thinking that the Earth would always fix whatever human beings did to it.

Nelson became more and more concerned over what he observed around the United States. Factories spewed out dirty smoke, rivers were

A strong believer in physical fitness, Senator William Proxmire used to run five miles to work every day, from his Washington home to his office. Once he even jogged all the way around Wisconsin, a run of 1,200 miles. This fast-paced senator first won election in 1957 and retired in 1989. While in the Senate, he worked hard to end wasteful governmental spending.

polluted, and valuable open space was lost to the spread of shopping malls and housing developments. He took a page from the anti-Vietnam War movement and decided to organize a "teach-in" about the environment. He called the event Earth Day.

Nelson and his supporters spent weeks seeking help for his idea from legislators, union officials, teachers, and business leaders. Finally, his efforts paid off. Twenty million people were estimated to have attended the first Earth Day celebrations on April 22, 1970. Since then, the annual event is a good reminder to all of us that it takes a lot of effort to protect the environment.

In 1980, Nelson became a legal advisor to the Wilderness Society and has remained active in many environmental causes since then. In honor of his efforts to save the environment, Nelson was awarded the Presidential Medal of Freedom, one of the country's highest civilian awards. He is an honored member of the Wisconsin Environmental Hall of Fame. ◆

Gaylord Nelson

Les Paul (b. 1916)

musician

Les Paul was always ahead of his time in developing technology for the music industry. Many techniques he developed are used today in rock and roll, jazz, and pop. These include phrase shifting, overdubbing, reverb, delay, and sound-on-sound recording. He also invented the popular eight-track guitar called the Gibson Les Paul.

In addition, Paul sold more than 10 million copies of his albums. He was still writing music and working on new musical techniques into his seventies.

Paul was born on June 9, 1916, in Waukesha, Wisconsin. At age nine, he built his first radio set. As a teenager, he played guitar and harmonica under the nickname of Rhubarb Red. When Paul performed at outdoor concerts, he wanted the audience to hear him better. So he figured that by sticking a phonograph needle inside a guitar and hooking it up to his radio, the sound would be amplified. When he was 13, he constructed a broadcasting station and built his own recording gear.

Paul started his professional career in a country-and-western band and performed at the Chicago World's Fair in the early 1930s. He stayed in

Les Paul

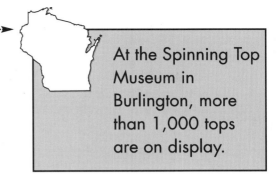

At the Spinning Top Museum in Burlington, more than 1,000 tops are on display.

Chicago, acting as a disc jockey in the morning and performing in jazz clubs and on the radio at night. He invented another type of guitar, one with strings that vibrated better and longer than any others on the market.

Paul traveled to New York and landed a job with the Fred Waring orchestra on NBC radio. When that ended in 1940, he came back to Chicago to be the musical director for several radio stations. Paul traveled often to California, meeting other famous instrument makers such as Paul Bigsby and Leo Fender. The two used many ideas suggested by the Wisconsin musician to improve their guitars.

During World War II, Paul performed for Armed Services Radio. He backed up such famous singers as the Andrews Sisters and Bing Crosby.

Things were looking up for Paul until 1948, when his right arm was crushed in an auto accident. Rather than have the arm amputated, he had the doctors permanently set the limb in a position that allowed him to still play the guitar. Soon afterwards, he met and married Colleen Summer, who changed her name to Mary Ford and became his singing partner for years. They had their own television show and recorded many hits together. Paul continued to work on his musical inventions and wrote sound tracks for several television series. He was even the musical director for the popular hit *Happy Days*.

Even with all this work, he continued to play regularly in nightclubs and to record, earning 22 gold records and many other music awards over his career. One of them was being named to the Rock and Roll Hall of Fame. He rightly earned the nickname the Wizard of Waukesha for his influence on music. ◆

Liberace (1919–1987)

entertainer

Liberace was "Mister Showman" to generations of fans who loved his piano skills, wild clothes, and lifestyle. One of his trademarks was a candelabra that was always on top of his piano when he performed. Liberace even made a model of this large candlestick holder into a ring. His other flashy jewelry included a diamond-studded, piano-shaped gold wristwatch.

Wladziu Valentino Liberace was born on May 16, 1919, in West Allis, a Milwaukee suburb. Wladziu is Polish for Walter. After he began to play music professionally, he changed his named to Liberace because it was easier to remember. His closest friends always called him Lee.

Liberace's family was very musical. His Italian father, Salvatore L.

Liberace

Liberace, played the French horn in the Milwaukee Symphony. His Polish mother, Frances Zuchowski, came from a long line of musicians, although she was not a musician like her husband. Liberace was often joined on stage by his brother, George, a very talented violinist.

Liberace began studying music when he was only 4 years old. When he was a little more than 7, he won a scholarship to the Wisconsin College of Music. This helped him continue his

studies for 17 years under the watchful eye of Florence Bettray-Kelly, who helped him prepare for the concert circuit. He got his first job at age 10, playing the piano in a show called "Milwaukee on Parade" at the fancy Alhambra Theater in Milwaukee.

While in high school, he joined a group called The Mixers and performed in nightclubs around Milwaukee, sometimes making only five dollars a night. When he was at the peak of his career, Liberace earned hundreds of thousands of dollars for each show. He became one of the country's highest paid performers of the 1960s and 1970s. In addition to his concert appearances, Liberace appeared in movies and television. He owned several homes and fancy cars, numerous dogs and, of course, loads of fancy clothes.

His costumes were a big part of his act. "It's part of the showmanship that I rely on. The clothes attract attention. They get me newspaper headlines and interviews. They get me audiences," he wrote in his biography. He often wore mink coats, ruffled cuffs on his shirts, and jeweled pants.

Liberace traveled many times around the world, performing in front of presidents and princesses, in addition to his regular audiences. They all loved his musical talent, as well as his wild dress. He went out of his way to please people. Once, when he gave a performance aboard an ocean liner, he insisted that all the passengers, not just those in first class, be allowed to attend.

Liberace died on February 4, 1987, at his mansion in Palm Springs, California. ◆

Vel Phillips (b. 1924)

social activist

Vel Phillips is used to being first. She did not plan it that way but was always in the right place at the right time. And more important, she had all the talent, creativity, and ambition needed to be a success.

Phillips was the first African-American and the first woman alderperson on the Milwaukee Common Council. She was also the first woman elected as Wisconsin secretary of state, making her the first African-American to hold statewide office. She was also the first woman of her heritage to receive a University of Wisconsin law degree and the first African-American elected to the Democratic National Committee. In addition, she was the first African-American judge in Wisconsin.

Vel Phillips

Phillips was born Vel Rogers on February 18, 1924, in Milwaukee. Even as a youngster, she wanted to be a lawyer, enjoying the give and take of debate. When she was a student at North Division High School, Phillips won a national speaking award from the Elks. This is an organization of businesspeople that sponsors charitable and social causes. Her speaking skills earned her a four-year scholarship to Howard University in Washington, D.C. The school is sometimes called the "Black

In 1996, Shirley Abrahamson became the first woman to be named chief justice of the Wisconsin Supreme Court.

Harvard" because of its excellent reputation educating African-Americans.

Phillips graduated from Howard in 1946 with a degree in social work. She then went on for her master's degree, meeting her future husband, law student Dale Phillips. The couple was married in 1948 and attended law school together at the University of Wisconsin-Madison.

When the two received their degrees in 1951, they went into law practice together in Milwaukee. The Phillipses were highly respected for their legal work. In 1955, Mr. Phillips decided to run for city alderman but dropped out. He encouraged his wife to run in his place. She worked hard to get out the votes and won, serving for the next 15 years.

Phillips was elected to the Democratic National Committee in 1958 and often represented the United States on overseas missions, especially to Africa. Always leading the push for equal rights for minorities, Phillips was active in Milwaukee's equal rights movement in the 1960s. She used her political position as alderperson to good advantage. But this did not always help. Phillips was arrested once for participating in an open-housing march.

She was named a judge in Milwaukee County's Children's Court in 1972 and elected secretary of state in 1978. In that position, she often served in place of the governor when he and lieutenant governor were out of the state. Phillips wanted to run for the U.S. Congress but dropped out of the race in 1988 when her husband died.

Phillips has won numerous awards over the years for her work. A YWCA building in Milwaukee is also named after her. ♦

William H. Rehnquist (b. 1924)
Supreme Court justice

Everyone who watched the impeachment trial of President Bill Clinton in 1999 saw William H. Rehnquist in action. As chief justice of the U.S. Supreme Court, Rehnquist presided over (served as the supreme authority in) the Clinton case. Wearing his black flowing robes, Rehnquist made quite an impression on the television audience.

Nominated to the highest court in the land by President Richard Nixon in 1971, Rehnquist is the only Wisconsin native to have been given this honor. In 1986, he became chief justice on the recommendation of President Ronald Reagan.

Born in Milwaukee on October 1, 1924, Rehnquist attended Atwater School and Shorewood High School. He was a good student, but some of his classmates thought him too serious. Yet other friends knew he could have a good time when he wanted to. His father was a sales director and his mother translated foreign languages.

William Rehnquist

Rehnquist always wanted to be a lawyer and enrolled in Harvard University to major in political science. During World War II, he joined the Army Air Corps and served from 1943 to

In 1911, Wisconsin passed the first law in U.S history that required employers to pay for injuries that workers suffered on the job. This resulted in safer working conditions and paved the way for similar laws in other states.

1946. When he was released he went back to college at Stanford University in California.

A bachelor's degree was not enough for Rehnquist, so he kept going on to earn two master's degrees. He graduated at the top of his law school class in 1952. With his fine academic record, he became a law clerk for Supreme Court Justice Robert H. Jackson. After two years, Rehnquist struck out on his own.

He moved to Phoenix, Arizona, to set up private practice. He worked there until being named an assistant attorney general in Washington, D.C. His legal advice to the president and other high government officials was very valuable.

When he was nominated, not everyone wanted to see Rehnquist become a Supreme Court justice. Some people thought he was too conservative and against too many important social causes. He had to defend his views in his nomination hearings in the Senate. Despite what some critics felt, Rehnquist received support from both Democrats and Republicans. They said that his legal abilities were more important than his political views.

Rehnquist is known to be very careful in writing his opinions for the Supreme Court. He presents clear arguments for or against whatever case he is studying.

It is interesting to note that in 1992 he wrote a historical account of the impeachment trial of President Andrew Johnson, which occurred in 1868. So, Rehnquist had a lot of insights about the impeachment process when he served as judge in the Clinton trial. ◆

John Colt (1925–1999)

artist

Dragonflies! Lizards! Beetles!

John Colt, one of Wisconsin's most important artists, loved painting the insect world. But he took nature and made it abstract, that is, showed it in new and wonderful ways. His paintings include those of a four-foot-wide dragonfly and of a squash that looks like the far side of the moon.

Colt was born on May 25, 1925, in Madison and died on April 27, 1999, in Amherst, Massachusetts, where he had retired. During his time as a teacher in Wisconsin, he was considered one of the state's finest artists. For 33 years, he was an art professor at the University of Wisconsin-Milwaukee.

John Colt

His father, Arthur, managed Madison's Colt School of Art for 40 years, giving his son valuable insights into the art world. After serving as an electrician on a submarine in the U.S. Navy during World War II, Colt earned a bachelor's degree in art education. He also earned a master's degree in art from the University of Wisconsin-Madison.

As a young man, Colt drove through the Wisconsin countryside on his way to his job teaching crafts to retired people in the town of Richland Center. On these trips, he became interested in the cycles of life and eagerly studied the natural world around him. He then visited Australia to teach high school art and returned to teach rehabilitation crafts in Janesville. From there, he joined the staff at the old Layton School of Art in Milwaukee.

In 1957, Colt began teaching at the University of Wisconsin-Milwaukee and was a visiting art professor at universities in Michigan and Indiana. He also made many visits overseas to continue painting and teaching. He often returned to Australia, and he taught at the American University in Beirut, Lebanon, and at the University of Saskatchewan in Canada. He sought additional inspiration in Mexico, the Bahama Islands, and Haiti. Occasionally, Colt used Native American themes in his paintings, often drawing medicine bundles and dolls.

Colt painted with oils, acrylics, watercolors, and pastels. He devised a method of thinning his paint and working on huge canvasses that lay on the floor. He sometimes used a sponge, as well as a paintbrush, in creating his marvelous pieces.

Colt's paintings, drawings, and prints of his snails, moths, tree stumps, vines, and seashells have been displayed in more than 100 shows around the country. Among the galleries that have showed his work are the Art Institute of Chicago, the Library of Congress in Washington, D.C., and the Whitney Museum in New York City. The 1994 calendar of the University of Wisconsin-Milwaukee featured his works. ♦

James Lovell (b. 1928)

astronaut

Seven-hundred and fifteen hours, plus five minutes—almost a month. That is how much time astronaut James Lovell spent in space. That is a long time, no matter what the situation. But during the four missions Captain Lovell was in space, every minute probably seemed like an eternity.

Born on March 25, 1928, in Cleveland, Ohio, he always wanted to fly in space and built model rockets as a youngster. Lovell moved with his mother to Milwaukee in 1935, attending Story School and graduating from Solomon Juneau High School in 1946. Lovell attended the University of Wisconsin-Madison from 1946 to 1948, hoping to play football. But he was considered too light, weighing only 155 pounds.

He enrolled in the naval officers' training program at the university

James Lovell

and then entered the U.S. Navy. There, Lovell did what he always wanted to do: fly. And he did it well. He did it so well that in September 1962, the National Aeronautics and Space Administration (NASA) selected him to be an astronaut. At first, he was a backup pilot. Lovell's big break came on December 4, 1965, when he was launched into space on the Gemini 7 mission. In November 1966, as the commander of Gemini 12, he orbited the earth 59 times with pilot Edwin Aldrin.

Between December 21 and 27, 1968, Lovell served as command module pilot and navigator on Apollo 8, the first manned spacecraft to leave the Earth's gravity pull and to reach the moon. Between April 11 and April 17, 1970, Lovell was commander of the Apollo 13 spacecraft. That trip was to prove his greatest challenge in space.

Along with crew members Jack Swigert and Fred Haise, Lovell was to land Apollo 13 on the moon, NASA's third such mission. But about halfway into the flight, there was an explosion in the service module. The craft lost oxygen and fuel. The goal of the trapped crew was now to get back to Earth as fast as possible. Lovell's wife, Marilyn, their four children, and the rest of the world waited breathlessly as he and his crew in space and NASA technicians on the ground worked to repair the problems.

The rest is history. The crew of Apollo 13 made a safe splashdown. Lovell retired from the astronaut program in 1971 and went on to become the chairman of the national Physical Fitness Council, appointed by President Richard Nixon. After that, Lovell managed a tugboat company before heading a communications firm. In the 1990s, he formed Lovell Communications to manage his speaking engagements and became a partner in a Chicago-area restaurant with his son, Jay, an executive chef.

But those tense hours in 1970, which he recorded in his book *Lost Moon*, remain probably the most challenging of his life. The 1995 movie *Apollo 13*, with Tom Hanks playing Lovell, showed just how dangerous the mission was.

Milwaukee has honored Lovell in several ways. Discovery World, next to the Milwaukee Public Museum, is also named the James Lovell Museum of Science, Economics, and Technology. The former astronaut attended the ribbon-cutting ceremony in 1996. At the same time, Milwaukee's 7th street outside the museum was renamed James Lovell Street. ◆

Father James Groppi (1930–1985)
social activist

Father James Groppi was a leader in Wisconsin's 1960s civil rights movement and a union activist in the 1970s and 1980s. Born on November 16, 1930, he was concerned about racism even as a young man growing up on Milwaukee's South Side. Groppi was one of 12 children in an Italian immigrant family. His father operated a grocery store.

Groppi always worried about poverty in Milwaukee. He figured that being a priest would be the best way to help the poor. He attended the seminary and was ordained a priest, becoming assistant pastor of Milwaukee's St. Boniface Catholic Church in 1963. The church, with its large black population, was a center for civil rights activities at the time.

When Groppi saw that many people, especially African-Americans, were not treated equally, he wanted to do something about it. In 1965, he went to Selma, Alabama, to march with the Reverend Martin Luther

Father James Groppi leading a protest march in Milwaukee

Before the Civil War, Wisconsin was an important link in the Underground Railroad. This was a network that provided shelter to runaway slaves on their way to Canada in search of freedom. One important stop on the railroad was the Milton House in the town of Milton, near Janesville. There, the Goodrich family cared for the runaways on their trip north.

King Jr. In 1966, he joined the March Against Fear, supporting voters' rights in the South.

Groppi always believed in peaceful protest and was saddened when a riot broke out in Milwaukee in 1967 in which several people were killed. Despite this, Groppi continued to lead his congregation in support of open housing, saying that people should be able to live anywhere they wished. Along with the Youth Council of the National Association for the Advancement of Colored People, he marched for 200 straight days for this important cause. Groppi was arrested many times, often while picketing the homes of Milwaukee aldermen to encourage them to pass an open-housing law.

The city rejected his pleas at least three times before finally agreeing to pass the law in the spring of 1968. Following Milwaukee's example, more than 50 other Wisconsin cities did the same.

Groppi was not about to sit still, even with this victory. He became a leader in the protests against the Vietnam War and led a demonstration in the State Capitol building in Madison. He resigned from St. Boniface in 1970, saying that it was important for an African-American priest to serve in an African-American parish. He went on to support Native American causes and other social issues.

He left the priesthood in 1976 to marry, working as a bus driver to support his family. Groppi became the president of the local bus drivers' union in 1983. The following year, he had cancer surgery but died on November 4, 1985. After Groppi's death, even people who did not like his tactics praised him for his brave stand on social issues. ◆

Alan Ameche (1933–1988)

football player

That honor of being the first University of Wisconsin football player to win the Heisman Trophy belongs to Alan Dante Ameche. He was born in Kenosha on June 1, 1933. His parents, August and Elizabeth, were Italian immigrants. His dad worked in a factory when the young Ameche attended high school in Kenosha. Ameche earned all-state fame in football and also was a track and field star.

Ameche decided to attend the University of Wisconsin-Madison, where his athletic talents were quickly recognized. He was a big young man, standing six feet tall and weighing 215 pounds. Despite his size, Ameche was fast, earning him the nickname the Horse.

While playing for the Badgers, Ameche set a four-year school rushing record of 3,345 yards. In fact, this hard-running fullback averaged 4.8 yards every time he carried the ball. He ran for more than 100 yards in a game 16 times. In a game against Minnesota, he gained 200 yards.

He scored 25 touchdowns in 37 games during his college career, from 1951 to 1955. As was common in those days, Ameche played both on offense and defense (he was also a linebacker). He won many awards, including being named an all-American in 1954. He was

Alan Ameche

In 1999, Ron Dayne became the second University of Wisconsin player to win the Heisman Trophy. The bruising running back also broke the NCAA Division I record for total yards gained in a regular season, 6,397. Counting his four bowl appearances, Dayne ran for over 7,000 yards during his college career.

also was an academic all-American. That meant he was a good student and a good football player. He also was awarded the Walter Camp Trophy in 1953 and 1954, as well as the Heisman Trophy, the most important award in college football, in 1954. He graduated with a physical education degree.

After college, Ameche played for the Baltimore Colts in the National Football League. During his pro career from 1955 to 1960, he rushed for 4,045 yards in 964 carries. He scored 44 touchdowns and caught 101 passes. During his first year with the Colts, Ameche was named all-pro and the NFL's Rookie of the Year.

Ameche is best remembered for scoring the Colts' winning touchdown in a rough-and-tumble sudden-death NFL title game against the New York Giants in 1958. The Colts won that squeaker by a score of 23 to 17.

When Ameche retired, he opened several popular restaurants. After he sold them, he opened three indoor tennis clubs in Pennsylvania. Ameche was elected to the NFL Football Hall of Fame in 1975. He died of a heart attack in 1988. ♦

Henry Aaron (b. 1934)

baseball player

Henry Louis "Hammerin' Hank" Aaron is considered one of the greatest baseball players of all time. Much of Aaron's professional life was spent with the Milwaukee Braves and, later, with the Milwaukee Brewers. On April 18, 1974, he hit his 715th home run, which broke Babe Ruth's lifetime record. Before he retired, he reached the 755 mark, a record that still stands today. Aaron was a league leader in home runs in 1957, 1963, 1966, and 1967. These feats show how he earned his nickname.

But Aaron had a hard time at the start of his career. Born on February 5, 1934, in Mobile, Alabama, he grew to be a talented player. But he found that there were few opportunities for young African-

Henry Aaron

Americans in the white world of professional baseball. So he started his professional career with the Indianapolis Clowns, a Negro League team. A scout for the team had seen Aaron playing with the semipro Mobile Black Bears when he was still in high school. Aaron was offered a job, but his mother insisted he finish school before joining the Clowns.

When the Clowns were bought by the Boston Braves, Aaron played on the club's minor league teams in Eau

Claire, Wisconsin, and Jacksonville, Florida for two years. Most major league teams own minor league clubs, which help inexperienced players improve their skills before moving up.

In 1953, the Braves moved to Milwaukee and brought Aaron with them soon after that. At first, he played shortstop and then moved to the outfield. He became a great right fielder but he sometimes played left or center field. In addition, this talented ball player often filled in at first base.

It was not long before Aaron began breaking records and earning honors. In 1956 and 1959, he captured the National League batting championship. In 1957, his efforts helped the Braves win the World Series, and he was elected the league's most valuable player. During his career, he was named to 24 all-star teams. For Aaron's lifetime of excellence on the field, he was elected to the National Baseball Hall of Fame on August 1, 1982.

When the Braves left Milwaukee and moved to Atlanta in 1966, Aaron went with them. But he returned to Milwaukee in 1974, when he was traded to the Brewers, who had become the city's new major league team. He ended his career with the ball club in 1976, after hitting his record-setting 755th home run.

When Aaron finally retired, he went back to the Atlanta Braves as a vice-president. Long active in social work and in helping young African-Americans to study hard and set career goals, he also served on the national board of the National Association for the Advancement of Colored People. ♦

Ada Deer (b. 1935)

political activist

Ada Deer was the first woman to direct the Bureau of Indian Affairs, a federal government department that looks after Native Americans. This was a high honor for a person who lived in a log cabin without running water or electricity until she was 12! Deer was born on August 7, 1935, on the Menominee Indian Reservation in Keshena, Wisconsin. Her father worked in a lumber mill and her mother was a nurse.

Encouraged by her mother, Deer worked very hard in school to lift herself out of poverty. She attended Shawano High School, winning a tribal scholarship to attend the University of Wisconsin-Madison. Deer became the first member of the Menominee nation to earn a degree in social work from the university. She graduated in 1957.

Ada Deer

Knowing she needed more education, Deer went on to receive a master's degree in social work from Columbia University in New York City. This deed earned her more notice because she was one of the first Menominees ever to receive a graduate degree in any field. She became a social worker in New York City and went on to work in Minnesota and Wisconsin, as well as in Puerto Rico.

For many years, most Native Americans lived on reservations, where they received federal financial help, job training, and

There are many Native American nations living in Wisconsin. The largest are the Ho-Chunk, Potawatomi, Menominee, Ojibwa, Oneida, Sioux, and Kickapoo. According to the U.S. Census Bureau, there were 46,000 Native Americans living in Wisconsin in 1997. The bureau predicted that by 2025, there would be about 65,000 in the state. More than 75 percent live in northern and northeastern Wisconsin. About 18 percent live in Milwaukee County.

education assistance. But in the 1960s, the government began to end these programs, slowly cutting off financial aid. This caused great hardship for many Native Americans because they found it difficult to pay for services they once got for free. Deer was concerned that the Menominee were not getting the help they needed. So in 1970, she founded a group called the Determination of Rights and Unity for Menominee Shareholders (DRUMS), which sought to correct this situation.

Deer traveled many times to Washington, D.C., to talk with federal officials about the hard times that her people were facing. Her efforts paid off. The Menominee Reservation was reestablished by President Richard Nixon in 1973, and once again the reservation was getting federal support. Deer soon was elected tribal chairman and served from 1974 to 1976.

In addition to her work for the Menominee, Deer taught at the University of Wisconsin-Madison and was active in Democratic Party politics. She ran for the U.S. Congress in 1992 and won her party's primary election. However, she was defeated in the general election.

In 1993, Deer became assistant Interior Secretary for Native American Affairs, heading the Bureau of Indian Affairs. This job made her the highest-ranking Native American in the federal government.

She returned to teaching at the University of Wisconsin in Madison in 1998 and a year later was named to head its Department of Native American Studies. Over her career, Deer has won many awards, including being named Woman of the Year by the Girl Scouts in 1982. ♦

Al Jarreau (b. 1940)

jazz singer

The velvet voice of Milwaukee jazz singer Al Jarreau is one of the best in the business. He won two Grammy Awards as best male vocalist of the year, the highest honor a musician can receive. Jarreau is so good that he earned the nickname the Acrobat of Scat. Scat is singing in which made-up words are used to create a special musical effect. There is not a real word like "shun-diddly-do-wah," but the phrase sounds great when sung along with instrumental accompaniment.

Born on March 12, 1940, Jarreau was lucky to grow up in a family that loved music. His father, a minister, was an excellent singer. His mother played the piano. Jarreau loved church hymns and enjoyed other kinds of music as well. His interests ran from country and western to pop and rock. He grew more and more attracted to jazz and all its creative possibilities.

Yet at first, Jarreau never seriously thought about making music his career. Instead, he attended Ripon College in Ripon, Wisconsin, graduating in 1962. He received his master's degree from the University of Iowa in 1964. Jarreau then became a counselor for handicapped youngsters in San Francisco.

But he always had time for music, especially jazz. In

Al Jarreau

Twenty percent of the children attending school in Wausau are of Asian heritage. Most of them are of Hmong descent. The Hmong people began arriving in Wisconsin in the late 1970s. They were refugees from Southeast Asia who had fought for the United States in the Vietnam War.

addition to his teaching job, Jarreau often sang in clubs around San Francisco. He performed with many famous musicians. In 1968, the lure of entertaining grew so strong that he left his counselor's job and made music his full-time career. His talents were recognized from the beginning. He sang in many of the country's best-known nightclubs and at concerts. Although he had a lot of talent, he had a hard time landing a recording contract or a full-time singing job.

Jarreau returned to Milwaukee. Far from giving up, he organized his own jazz-rock band and continued writing lyrics. It was not long before the bright lights of the West Coast lured him back to Los Angeles. He performed in such well-known clubs as the Bla Bla Cafe. At the famous Troubadour nightspot, Mo Austin, the president of Warner Brothers Records, heard Jarreau on stage. Immediately, Austin signed the Wisconsin singer to record for his company. In 1975, Warner released Jarreau's first album, *We Got By*.

The record showed Jarreau's wide-ranging musical talents and set him on the road to success. He recorded nine more major albums by 1986 and numerous singles.

In addition to his Grammy Awards, Jarreau won many music honors in other countries. The German Music Academy named him the outstanding male vocalist in 1976. The Italian Music Critics Award gave him the nod as the best foreign vocalist for 1977. He always won rave notices from music industry magazines such as *down beat* and *Cash Box*.

Jarreau enjoys coming home to Milwaukee to visit his family. Sometimes, he even drops by a local club to sing a few songs. ◆

Eric Heiden (b. 1958)
& Beth Heiden (b. 1959)
speed skaters

Madison's Eric and Beth Heiden grew up in a family of skaters. Ever since they were little, this brother-and-sister pair was always on the ice. Even as youngsters, they belonged to skating clubs and competed in meets. Eric was born on June 14, 1958, and Beth was born on September 27, 1959.

This early training and many years of practice took them to the Olympics. In the 1980 Winter Games at Lake Placid, Eric won five gold medals, capturing the 500-, 1,000-, 1,500-, 5,000-, and 10,000-meter speed-skating events. Beth won a bronze medal in those games, taking third place in the 3,000-meter event.

Eric was trained by Dianne Holum, an Olympic speed-skating champion. A lot of Eric's training was taken up with riding a bicycle and lifting weights. This developed strong legs and endurance, the two most important things a speed skater needs.

Eric kept at his training. He was determined to become the fastest skater in the world. In 1975, Eric competed in his first international race, coming in 10th. Then, in the 1976 Winter Olympics, he earned 7th place in the 1,500-meter race and was 19th in the 5,000 meters.

Eric's talent carried him to the 1977 World Speed Skating Championships. At age 19, he became the first American to

Eric and Beth Heiden

In 1999, the *Milwaukee Journal-Sentinel* selected 25 of Wisconsin's top athletes. Among them were Ernie Nevers, of Superior, who once scored 40 points in a National Football League game. Burleigh Grimes, of Emerald, won 270 games as a major league pitcher. Johnny Revolta, Oshkosh, won 13 major tournaments as a professional golfer, including the 1935 PGA championship. Archie Hahn, Dodgeville, is only one of two sprinters in the world ever to win the 100-meter dash in back-to-back Olympics. He won four gold Olympic medals.

capture the overall title in the event's 76-year history. More titles and honors piled up. Eric soon won the World Sprint Championship and the World Junior Speed Skating Championship. Between 1977 and 1980, he captured nine other major international skating titles. After he won a third straight world overall title in Norway in 1979, the U.S. named him honorary sports ambassador to that country.

All this time, Beth was also doing very well. Participating in high school track as part of her skating training, she set a national record in the mile run. Also an excellent cyclist, she competed in many events. In 1979, the year before she captured her Olympic bronze medal in skating, she won the women's overall world cycling title. In 1980, she won the National Road Championship and swept the Coors International Classic.

In 1982, Beth tried her hand at skiing. She did as well in that sport as she had done in skating and biking. While at the University of Vermont, she captured an NCAA title for cross-country skiing.

Eric ended his competitive skating career after his five-medal Olympic sweep. He then also turned to cycling and participated in the 1986 Tour de France, the world's most important bike race. In 1990, he was elected to the Wisconsin Sports Hall of Fame and was named the male Winter Olympian of the Century by the Associated Press in 1999. Both Heidens certainly stand tall in the Wisconsin athletic world. ◆

Brett Favre (b. 1969)

football player

Football always meant everything to Green Bay Packers quarterback
Brett Favre. He got this attitude from his father, Irvin, a high school
football coach who encouraged and taught him well. Favre was born
on October 10, 1969, in the small town of Kiln, Mississippi. The story
goes that his home was so close to a body of swampy water called
Rotten Bayou that three of his pet dogs were eaten by alligators. And it
was always easy to go fishing. Favre could throw out a line from his
back porch to catch his supper.

As a player at the University of Southern Mississippi, Favre showed
much of the talent that was later to make him famous. He became the
team's starting quarterback in the third game of his freshman year and
went on to set several school records for passing. The skills and winning
attitude his father taught him were paying off. He was drafted by the
National Football League's Atlanta Falcons in 1991. But college ball was
different than playing for the pros. Unimpressed with his early
performance, the Falcons traded him to Green Bay in 1992.

The Packers recognized Favre's raw skills and talent, and he did not
disappoint them. When regular quarterback Don Majkowski was injured
in the third game of the 1992 season, Favre was called in. He did so well
that he has been Green Bay's starting quarterback ever since.

He has also become one of the top players in the NFL, being named
the league's Most Valuable Player in 1995, 1996, and 1997. He has led the
league in passing yards, completions, and touchdowns several times.
Favre is not only talented but also durable. In 1999, he set the NFL
record for the most starts in a row by a quarterback, 117, a number that
is increasing with every game he starts. His biggest victory was played
in 1997, when he led the Packers to a Super Bowl win over the New

England Patriots, 35-21. In that game, he tossed two touchdown passes
and ran for a third score. However, Favre and the Packers lost 31-24 to
Denver in the 1998 Super Bowl.

Favre's activities off the field are almost as well known as his
gridiron feats. Several years ago, he was treated for a minor addiction
to drugs and alcohol, and he has faced other challenges to his career.
But he recovered and has continued playing, delighting his many fans
across the country. ♦

Brett Favre

Index

A

Aaron, Henry, 96–97
Abrahamson, Shirley, 85
Academy Award (Oscar), 67
Albany, New York, 12
Aldrin, Edwin, 90
Algonquins (Native Americans), 3
Ameche, Alan, 94–95
American Academy of Dramatic Arts, 66
American Circus Corporation, 39
American Fur Company, 10, 11
American Library Association, 41
American Revolution, 7, 8
American Safety Razor Company
    (Gillette Safety Razor Co.), 29
Apollo 8, 13, 91,
Appleton, 44, 45, 54,
Appleton Crescent, 54
Army Corps of Engineers, 50
Art Institute of Chicago, 56
Art Students League, 56
Arkansas River, 5
Assiniboine (Native Americans), 2
Assippunion, 36
Atwater School, 86

B

Badger State, 27
Baldwin, Tammy, 37
The Ballot Box, 29
Baraboo, 39
Bardeen, John, 70–71
Barnes, Al G., 39
Barnum and Bailey Circus, 39
Bennett, H.H., 26–27
Big Manitou Falls, 25

Birth, 46
Black Hawk, 8–9
Black Hawk Unit (Lower Wisconsin
    Parkway), 9
Black Hawk War, 9
Bonga, George, 13
Bonga, Jean and Marie Jeanne, 12
Bonga, Pierre, 12
Bonga, Stephen, 12–13
Bonga Township, 13
Boys' Town, 67
Brandenstein, Daniel C., 91
Breese, William L., 47
The Bridge of San Luis Rey, 62
British, 6, 7, 12
Brown, Reverend Olympia, 37
Bureau of Indian Affairs, 98
Butternuts, New York, 16
By the Shores of Silver Lake, 40

C

The Cabala, 63
California, 25
Canada, 2, 6, 12, 25
The Captain of the Gray Horse Troop, 35
Carroll College, 60
Captains Courageous, 67
Case, Belle, 30
Cassville, 17
Catt, Carrie Chapman, 32–33
Catt, George William, 33
de Champlain, Samuel, 2
Channing, Carol, 61
Chapman, Leo, 33
Cherokees (Native Americans), 8
Chevalier, Bartelemi, 10

Chevalier, Marie, 10–11
Cigrand, Bernard, 69
Circus World Museum, 39
Citizen Kane, 76
Civil War, 19, 22, 26, 50
Clinton, President Bill, 86, 87
Communist Party, 68
Cold War, 68
Colt, John, 88–89
Communism, 68
The Court-Martial of Billy Mitchell, 49
Coward, Noel, 61
Crumbling Idols, 35

D

Dairy cattle, 23
Dane County, 30
A Daughter of the Middle Border, 35
Davidson, Arthur, 52
Davidson, Walter, 52
Davidson, William, 52
Dawn O'Hara, 54
Dayne, Ron, 95
Deer, Ada, 98–99
DePere, 5
Design for Living, 60
Determinations of Rights and Unity for
    Menominee Shareholders, 99
Dewey, Nelson, 16–17
Discovery World, 91
The Doctor's Dilemma, 60
Dunn, Charles, 17
Dunn, Kate, 17

E

Earth Day, 79
Eisenhower, President Dwight D., 69

F

Fanny Herself, 55
Farmer Boy, 40
Farnsworth, William, 11

Favre, Brett, 104–105
Fennimore Doll Museum, 39
Ferber, Edna, 54–55
Flag Day, 69
Fond du Lac, 28
Fontanne, Lynn, 60–61
Forest Home Cemetery, 21, 61
Fort Monroe, Virginia, 9
Fox River, 5, 59
Franks, Michael, 65
French, 6
French and Indian War of 1754, 6
French Revolution, 10

G

Gale, Zona, 46–47
Garland, Hamlin, 34–35
The Guardsman, 60
Gemini 7, 90
General Billy Mitchell International
    Airport, 49
Genesse Depot, 61
Gibson Les Paul, 80
Gillette, King Camp, 28–29
Gillette razor, 29
Gillette Safety Razor Company
    (American Safety Razor Company), 29
Gillette's Social Redemption, 29
glaciers, 15
Grammy Awards, 100, 102
Grand Chute, 69
Grant County, 16
Great Circus Parade, 39
Great Depression, 40, 50
Great Marten, 10
Green Bay, 3, 5, 6, 7, 10, 11, 20, 29, 83,
    104
Green Bay Intelligencer, 21
Green Bay Packers, 72, 73, 104, 105
Green Lake, 15
Grimes, Burleigh, 103
Groppi, Father James, 92–93

Guess Who's Coming to Dinner, 67
Gulf of Mexico, 25

H

Hagenbeck-Wallace Animal Show, 39
Haise, Fred, 91
Hahn, Archie, 103
Handcuff Secrets, 45
Happy Days, 81
Harding, Warren G., 48
Harley, William, 52–53
Harley-Davidson Motor Company, 53
Hayes, Helen, 61
Hearts's Kindred, 46
Heiden, Beth, 102–103
Heiden, Eric, 102–103
Heisman Trophy, 94
Hello, Dolly!, 63
Hepburn, Katharine, 61, 67
The Herd, 75
Herman, Woody, 74–75
Hmong, 101
Hoard, William Dempster, 22–23
Hoard's Dairyman, 23
Hoard Historical Museum and Dairy
    Shrine, 23
Ho-Chunk (Winnebago), 2, 27
hodag, 45
Holum, Diane, 102
Hoover, President Herbert, 51
Horning, Paul, 73
Houdini, Harry, 44–45
Houdini, 45
Houdini Historical Center, 45
Howard University, 84
The Human Drift, 29

I

Ice Age, 15
Idiot's Delight, 60
Illinois (state), 8
Illinois, (Native Americans), 2, 5

Iowa State College, 32
Israel, 64

J

Jacobs, John, 10
James Lovell Museum of Science,
    Economics and Technology, 91
Jarreau, Al, 100–101
Jefferson County Union, 22
Joan of Arc, 5
John and Mabel Ringling Art Museum,
    39
John Robinson, 39
Johnson, President Andrew, 87
Jolliet, Louis, 4
Jones-Lloyd, Anna, 42

K

Kenosha, 21, 76, 83, 94
Keshena, 98
kibbutz, 64
Korean War, 9, 51

L

Labor Zionist Party, 64
La Crosse, 34
La Follette, Robert M., 30–31
La Follette, Robert M. Jr., 31
Lake Geneva, 66
Lake Huron, 12
Lake Michigan, 5
Lake Winnebago, 15
Lancaster, 16
de Langlade, Charles Michel, 6–7
Langlade County, 7
Lapham, Increase Allen, 14–15
The Last Mile, 66
Layton School of Art, 89
Laura Ingalls Wilder Award, 41
League of Women Voters, 33
Lebanon, Connecticut, 16

Leopold, Aldo, 58–59
Liberace, 82–83
Light Woman, 47
Lincoln, Abraham, 19, 21, 30
Little House on the Prairie, 40
Little Town on the Prairie, 40
Lombardi, Vince, 72–73
Lost Moon, 91
Lovell, James, 90–91
Lunt, Alfred, 60–61

M

MacArthur, Douglas, 50–51
MacArthur Square, 51
Mackinac Island, 12
Madison, 30, 83, 88
Madison Square Garden, 39
Main-Traveled Roads, 34
A Magician Among the Spirits, 45
The Magnificent Yankee, 61
Majkowski, Don, 104
Manitowoc shipyard, 75
Marinette County, 11
Marquette, Father Jacques, 4–5
Marquette-Jolliet Expedition, 5
Marquette University, 5, 68
Marshall George, 69
Mason City, Iowa, 33
Mason City Republican, 33
The Matchmaker, 63
McCarthy, Joseph, 68–69
Medal of Honor, 9
Menominee (Native Americans), 98
Meir, Golda, 64–65
Menominee River, 10
"The Merchant of Yonkers", 63
Mercury Theatre Company, 77
Methodist Episcopal Church, 13
military outpost, 12
Milwaukee, 14, 15, 21, 47, 83, 84, 86, 91,
    93, 100, 101
    public library, 14, 47

Mexican ancestry, 57
Milwaukee Board of Public Works, 21
Milwaukee Braves, 96
Milwaukee Brewers, 96
Milwaukee Daily-Sentinel, 21
Milwaukee Journal, 54
Milwaukee News, 21
Milwaukee & St. Paul Railroad, 19
Milwaukee Public Museum, 91
Milwaukee Repertory Theater, 61
Milwaukee Teachers College, 64
Miss Lula Bett, 47
Minocqua, 37
Mississippi River, 4, 6, 8, 16, 40
Mitchell, Alexander, 18–19, 48
Mitchell, John L., 19, 48
Mitchell, Red Cloud, 9
Mitchell, William "Billy", 48–49, 50
Monona Terrace, 43
Mooresburg, Pennsylvania, 20
Mothers to Men, 47
Muir, John, 24–25
My Life, 65
Myerson, Morris, 64

N

19th Amendment, 32
National Association for the
    Advancement of Colored People,
    93, 97
Native Americans, 2, 15, 98, 99
National Aeronautics and Space
    Administration, 90
National Baseball Hall of Fame, 97
National Institute of Arts and Letters,
    57
National Weather Service, 14
Negro League, 96
Nelson, Gaylord, 78–79
Nevers, Ernie, 103
New York Evening World, 46
Newcomb, Dr. Kate Pelham, 37

NFL Football Hall of Fame, 72, 95
Nicolet, Jean, 2–3
19th Amendment, 32, 33, 36
Nipissing, 2
Nixon, President Richard, 86, 91
Nobel Prize, 70
North Division High School, 84
Northwest Fur Company, 12
Northwestern Military and Naval
    Academy, 66

O

O'Keefe, Georgia, 56–57
Oconomowoc Lake, 15
Ohio, 6
Ojibwa, 13
Old-Fashioned Tales, 47
Olivier, Laurence, 61
Olympics, 102
On the Banks of Plum Creek, 40
Osage, 8
Ottawa (Native Americans), 6
Ottawa River, 2
Our Town, 62

P

Palestine, 64, 65
Pattison State Park, 25
Paul, Les, 80–81
Peace in Friendship Village, 47
Pearl Harbor, 49
Pepin, 40–41
Perrot, Nicolas, 11
Perrot State Park, 11
Phillips, Vel, 84–85
Plankinton House, 50
Portage, 24, 46
Portage, Wisconsin, and Other Essays, 47
Potawatomi (Native Americans), 2
Presidential Medal of Freedom, 79
Prairie du Chien, 5
Primrose, 30
Progressives, 31

Proxmire, Senator William, 79
Pulitzer Prize, 35, 47, 55, 63

Q

Quadracci Powerhouse Theater, 67
Quebec, 2, 3

R

Racine, 43, 83
Red Cloud, Mitchell, 9
Reagan, President Ronald, 86
Rehnquist, William H., 86–87
Remington Arms Company, 21
Revolta, Johnny, 103
Richland Center, 42
Ringling brothers (Charles, Albert C.,
    Alfred T., Otto, A.G., Henry), 38–39
Ringling Brothers Circus, 38, 39,
Ringling, John R., 38–39
Ripon, 32
Ripon College, 66, 100
RKO Pictures, 77
Robertson, Daniel, 12
Romance Island, 46
Roosevelt, President Franklin, 59
Roosevelt, President Theodore, 25
Rose of Dutcher's Coolly, 35
R.U.R., 66

S

S.C. Johnson and Son Wax Company, 43
SS Meteor, 13
Sac (Sauk) nation, 8
St. Boniface Catholic Church, 92
A Sand County Almanac, 59
scat singing, 100
Scotland, 18, 24
The Seagull, 60
Sells-Floto, 39
The Shadow, 77
The Shadow World, 35
Shawano High School, 98

110

A Son of the Middle Border, 35
Shenandoah, 49
Shephard, Eugene, 45
Sherwood, Robert, 61
Sholes, Christopher Latham, 20–21
Shorewood High School, 86
Show Boat, 55
Sioux, (Native Americans), 2, 8, 9, 13
The Skin of Our Teeth, 63
Snake River, 13
So Big, 55
Solomon Juneau High School, 90
Spanish, 5
Spanish-American War, 48, 50
Sparks Circus, 39
Special Commission on Wildlife Restoration, 59
Spinning Top Museum, 81
St. Croix River, 13
St. Francis Xavier Mission, 5
St. Ignace, Michigan, 4, 5
Starr, Bart, 73
State Historical Society of Wisconsin, 14, 17, 27
Stevens, Brooks, 89
Stieglitz, Alfred, 57
Stockbridge, New York, 22
Story School
The Story of My Boyhood and Youth, 24
Straits of Mackinac, 12
Success, 46
suffrage movement, 32
Summer, Colleen (Mary Ford), 81
Sun Prairie, 56
Super Bowl, 72, 73, 104, 105
Superior, 12, 13
Swigert, Jack, 91

T

Taliesin East, 43
The Taming of the Shrew, 60
Ten Chimneys, 61
Thompson, Governor Tommy, 9, 17

Those Happy Golden Years, 40
Timm's Hill, 43
Tour de France, 103
Tracy, Spencer, 66–67
trading post, 6, 10, 11
Truman, President Harry, 51
typewriter, 20

U

Underground Railroad, 93
United States Military Academy, West Point, 50
University of Wisconsin Board of Regents, 23, 47
University of Wisconsin-Madison, 25, 30, 42, 46, 59, 70, 71, 77, 84, 90, 94, 98
University of Wisconsin Law School, 78, 85
University of Wisconsin Medical School, 70
University of Wisconsin-Milwaukee, 88, 89
University of Wyoming, 33
Utah, 25
U.S. Supreme Court, 86, 87

V

Vietnam War, 93
The Visit, 60

W

The War of the Worlds, 76
Washington, D.C., 5, 31
Waukesha, 80
Waukesha Freeman, 36
Wells, Orson, 76–77
We Got Bye, 101
West Allis, 82, 83, 105
West Division High School, 50
Whigs, 19
Wilder, Almanzo James, 40
Wilder, Laura Ingalls, 40–41
Wilder, Thornton, 62–63, 67

Wilderness Society, 79
Wilson, President Woodrow, 33
Wisconsin, 3, 16, 19, 22, 23, 24, 38
   Asian heritages, 101
   bird, 31
   cheese production, 23,
   colleges and universities, 63
   dog, 31
   ethnic groups, 55, 101
   farms, 41
   flag, 31
   flower, 31
   governors, 17
   highway, 53
   household income, 51
   idea, 31
   insect, 31
   libraries, 35
   miners, 27
   motto, 31
   paper products, 29
   territory, 6, 15
   territorial legislature, 20, 21
   tree, 31
   universities, 63
Wisconsin Banker's Association, 18

Wisconsin College of Music, 82
Wisconsin Division of Tourism, 5
Wisconsin Free Library Commission, 47
Wisconsin Dells, 26, 27
Wisconsin Women's Suffrage
   Association, 37
Wisconsin Marine & Fire Insurance
   Company, 18
Wisconsin Heights battlefield, 9
Wisconsin River, 5, 25
WHA radio, 77
Wolcott, Laura Ross, 37
Women's Suffrage, 33, 36
"Woodchopper's Ball", 74
Woody Herman Music Archives, 75
World War I, 29, 48, 50, 66
World War II, 51, 62, 65, 68, 69, 71, 75,
   81, 86
Wright, Frank Lloyd, 42–43
Wright, Orville, 48
Wright, William, 42

Y

Yale University, 58
Yosemite Valley, 25
Youmans, Theodora, 36–37

Photo Credits

Pages 3,WHi (X3) 30553; 4, WHi (X3) 23784; 8, WHi (X3) 51484; 10, WHi (X3) 35393; 16, WHi (X3) 30479; 18, WHi (X3) 22632; 20, WHi (X313) 2564; 22, WHi (X3) 9549; 24, WHi (X3) 8173; 26, BF-17; 30, WHi (X3) 45820; 32, WHi (X3) 42033; 34, WHi (X3) 32275; 36, WHi (X313) 2816; 38, WHi (X3) 52519; 42, WHi (D479) 12495; 46, WHi (X3) 15040; 48, WHi (X28) 4176; 54, WHi (X3) 43390; 60, WHi (X3) 2373; 62, WHi (X3) 2538; 68, WHi (X3) 19886; 79, WHi (X3) 47150; 84, WHi (X3) 32911; 92, WHi (X3) 36107. Courtesy of the State Historical Society of Wisconsin.

Page 7. Courtesy of the Neville Public Museum.

Pages 44, 66, 74, 76, 82, 100. Courtesy of the Wisconsin Center for Film and Theater Research.

Page 13. Courtesy of the Superior (Wis.) Public Library.

Pages 14 and 80. Courtesy of the Waukesha County Historical Museum.

Page 28. Courtesy of the Gillette Company.

Page 41. Courtesy of the Laura Ingalls Wilder Home Association, Mansfield, Missouri.

Page 51. Courtesy of the Milwaukee County Historical Society.

Page 52. Courtesy of the Harley-Davidson Motor Company Archives.

Pages 56, 64, 72, 86, 88, 94, 96, 98, 102, 105. Courtesy of the Milwaukee Journal Sentinel.

Page 58. Photo by Robert Oetking. Courtesy of the University of Wisconsin-Madison Archives.

Page 70. AP/Worldwide Photos.

Page 90. Courtesy of NASA.

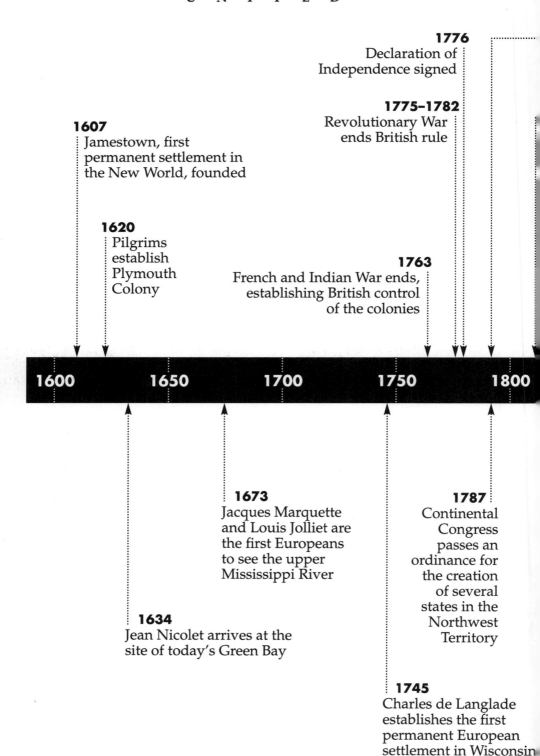

U N I T E D

1776
Declaration of
Independence signed

1775–1782
Revolutionary War
ends British rule

1607
Jamestown, first
permanent settlement in
the New World, founded

1620
Pilgrims
establish
Plymouth
Colony

1763
French and Indian War ends,
establishing British control
of the colonies

| 1600 | 1650 | 1700 | 1750 | 1800 |

1673
Jacques Marquette
and Louis Jolliet are
the first Europeans
to see the upper
Mississippi River

1787
Continental
Congress
passes an
ordinance for
the creation
of several
states in the
Northwest
Territory

1634
Jean Nicolet arrives at the
site of today's Green Bay

1745
Charles de Langlade
establishes the first
permanent European
settlement in Wisconsin

W I S C O N S I N